RUPTURED

JEWISH WOMEN
IN AUSTRALIA
REFLECT ON LIFE
POST-OCTOBER 7

RUPTURED

JEWISH WOMEN
IN AUSTRALIA
REFLECT ON LIFE
POST-OCTOBER 7

EDITED BY
LEE KOFMAN &
TAMAR PALUCH

PRAISE FOR *RUPTURED*

'The silence of so many non-Jewish Australians about rising antisemitism in Australia after the horror of the October 7 pogrom by Hamas, and the failure to reach out to comfort long-term Jewish friends and colleagues, has broken the hearts and trust of many Jewish women. These marvellous, powerful and heartbreaking essays offer open-hearted readers the opportunity to understand the distress of Jewish women and talk to their Jewish friends and colleagues about counteracting Jew-hatred in Australia.'

Julie McCrossin AM

'The title says it all – these are cries of pain, of disillusion, of loss of lifelong friendships, of search for identity, and above all, of shattering of trust and confidence. But these are also triumphant voices – of hope, strength, courage, of resilience and reconnection with roots and community. A Magen David reclaimed, a cherished family recipe shared, a renewal of faith, and a voice and a tribe rediscovered. At the end of each essay, I wanted to reach out and embrace the woman who had crafted those words so fearlessly and with such honesty. Such small threads, but together they weave a tapestry of fearlessness and of dreams for a better world.'

Nina Bassat AM

'By turns hopeful, thoughtful, grieving and painful, these essays by Australian Jewish women challenge us to move beyond our own beliefs, perceptions and context to that place where simple binaries open out into the many-coloured, multi-faceted, lived experiences of others.'

Robyn Cadwallader, author of *The Fire and the Rose*

'There are some events which forever change those they touch. The attacks of October 7, 2023, and their aftermath have reverberated around the world, felt keenly in communities everywhere. In capturing the perspectives of Australian Jewish women, *Ruptured* provides an important new lens. Horror and grief intersect with resilience and determination through these pages, in a text which deserves a place among the chronicles of this complicated history.'

Meg Kenneally, author of *Free*

'Contemporary terrors collide with unimaginable histories in this raw, courageous and unflinching collection from some of Australia's finest writers.'

Van Badham, author of *QAnon and On*

'This book is a moving and thoughtful intervention by Jewish women of all political stripes into the unhinging polarisation of the social media age and the resurgence of antisemitism. Read it before you judge it.'

Professor Catharine Lumby, author of *Frank Moorhouse*

'Fissured between these pages are necessary voices of pertinacious strength, unwavering courage, solidarity, womanhood, survival and faith – matrilineal, intergenerational, umbilical; Jewish Australian women here and now refuse to be de facto to a united global cloak of denial and silence. Giving rise to their shared essays, thirty-six women bring forth an ancient lantern of light and resilience through the gift of language. Their stories will pause you, conflict you – dare I suggest, embrace you. To be pierced is to be ruptured. To be ruptured is to overcome. To overcome is to heal.'

Yvette Henry Holt, Australian Literary Executive and author of *Fitzroy North 3068*

'A testimony of – and testament to – our community's resilience. You will be gripped; you will be galvanised. You will know you're not alone.'

Alice Zaslavsky, author of *Salad for Days*

'*Ruptured* is a raw, urgent, and deeply moving collection of stories from over 30 Jewish women in Australia, each navigating life in the wake of October 7. From cultural icons like Deborah Conway to young voices like Noa Gomberg, these women lay bare their fears, their pain, and their resilience in the face of an alarming rise in antisemitism. Their words are harrowing yet necessary – a testament to survival, identity, and the enduring strength of Jewish women who have contributed so much to this country. This book is essential reading for all Australians, particularly women, and women's groups, to truly grasp the depth of what these women have endured. I urge every reader to listen, learn, and stand against hatred in all its forms.'

Nova Peris OAM OLY

'*A person can endure anything as long as they can write a book about it.*'

Shifra Horn, *Scorpion Dance*

First published in 2025 by Lamm Jewish Library of Australia (LJLA)
www.ljla.org.au

ISBN: 9780646714363
ISBN: 9780646714370 (eBook)

Text © Individual contributors 2025

Early versions of/excerpts from featured essays by Lisa Goldberg, Elana Benjamin, Jessica Bowker, Kylie Moore Gilbert, Ramona Koval & Lee Kofman were first published in *The Jewish Independent*.

The moral rights of the individual contributors have been asserted.

All rights reserved. No part of this publication may be reproduced, published, performed in public or communicated to the public in any form or by any means without prior written permission from the publisher.

 A catalogue record for this work is available from the National Library of Australia

Authors: Lee Kofman & Tamar Paluch
Editorial support & production management: Romy Moshinsky
Project management: Simonne Whine
Publishing support: Dr Rolene Lamm (chair, LJLA) & Dr Merav Carmeli (director, LJLA)
Design & typesetting: Marianna Berek-Lewis, 5678 Design
Cover image: © Akkash Vertical – Adobe Stock

Proceeds from sales of *Ruptured* will support further distribution of the book and the vital work of the Lamm Jewish Library of Australia, which serves as a comprehensive national resource centre on Jewish life, literature and history, the Holocaust, and Israel; and as a cultural and educational hub for the Australian community.

We respectfully acknowledge the traditional custodians of the land this book is published on – the Bunurong, Boonwurrung and Wurundjeri Woi Wurrung Peoples of the Kulin nation. We pay our respects to First Nations Elders past, present and emerging.

Printed in Australia by McPherson's Printing Group

CONTENTS

INTRODUCTION   12

A Stone Under History's Wheel **Ramona Koval**   18

Pickle Project **Elise Esther Hearst**   26

I am a Jew **Irena Zilberman**   31

We Are Still Here **Mindy Sotiri**   37

The End of Ignorance **Noa Gomberg**   44

Against Silence **Julia Meyerowitz-Katz**   48

Nana's Bracelet **Jemima Montag**   55

The Privilege of Being a Pacifist **Joanne Fedler**   59

What Hurts More? **Kerri Sackville**   67

Who Will Hide My Daughter? **Galit Klas**   74

The Crack and the Light **Melinda Jones**   79

A Rant and a Recipe **Lisa Goldberg**   86

Pacing the Stage **Deborah Conway**   92

Police Report **Nina Sanadze**	99
In Case I Ever Get Kidnapped **Tamar Paluch**	104
Nothing Antisemitic Here **Nicky Stein**	111
Open Hiding **Dani Valent**	116
Writing in the Time of War **Lee Kofman**	120
Boiled Eggs **Ruby Kraner-Tucci**	129
Walls **Kylie Moore-Gilbert**	136
The Pain of Others **Lynette Chazan**	139
Faith Over Fear **Dena Amy Kaplan**	147
October 7 Diary **Julie Szego**	151
North of the River **Siana Einfeld**	160
(Un)safe **Kate Lewis**	167
Hanging on by a Thread **Sidra Kranz Moshinsky**	172
The Winner **Lana Schwarcz**	178
Warrior of Words **Sharonne Blum**	191
My Kitchen Sanctuary **Elana Benjamin**	194
The Woman in the Arena **Simonne Whine**	201
A Daily Update **Kim Rubenstein**	207
The Women's Circle **Sharon Sztar**	213

And Still We Dance **Rabbi Jacqueline Ninio**	**218**
Jewish Enough **Noè Harsel**	**222**
A Message from My Friend **Jessica Bowker**	**227**
I'm Not Antisemitic, But… **Rachelle Unreich**	**234**
CONTRIBUTORS	**240**
ACKNOWLEDGEMENTS	**247**

INTRODUCTION

'I have no words,' says a well-known novelist when we invite her to write an essay about how her life has changed since the Hamas attack on Israeli civilians, the subsequent Israel-Hamas war and the explosion of antisemitism globally. 'I've not written a thing since October 7.' She, the wordsmith, has had no words for over a year now.

Another creative woman with a public profile has the words. They are sharp and sad and vulnerable, and occasionally darkly funny. She sends her essay to us, then withdraws it. She is fearful of the repercussions. And why wouldn't she be? Speaking, and writing, as a Jew has become a dangerous act. (Ironic, given how many Jewish writers are part of the literary canon, even though Jews make up just 0.2 percent of the world's population.) 'When I spoke up online, I faced abuse, daily,' writes one of our contributors, the actress, singer and dancer Dena Amy Kaplan. 'I lost half of my following on Instagram. I lost friends – many of them. I lost work opportunities, and my career stalled.' As a result, she 'stopped speaking out publicly about Israel and being Jewish because I couldn't handle the emotional toll... It was no longer safe for me to be Jewish in the public eye – a tragedy, considering how proud I am of my heritage.'

Life has irrevocably changed for Jews in this country of the 'fair go'. Even before October 7, our institutions and events were always under threat, always had to be guarded. Yet many of us didn't give this too much thought; we felt like we belonged here. In the year following October 7, antisemitic activity in Australia increased by 316 percent.[1] One in five Australians now holds antisemitic attitudes (the highest rate across the Anglosphere nations)[2], and these so-called attitudes are no longer confined to private thoughts, nor even to online spaces where Jew-hatred is thriving, unchecked and normalised. As we write these words in February 2025, the real-life violence continues to escalate. The world around us is burning. Like, literally burning – cars, synagogues, even a childcare centre was recently firebombed in Sydney. And the feeling among Jewish people in Australia, as the essays in this book reveal, is that of a profound existential rupture.

'I have to remember what life was like before October 7 and that's hard to do. It is like trying to remember a faded romance or the texture of life when I was at high school,' journalist Julie Szego writes. Some women now sense an invisible barrier separating them from most other Australians, those without personal ties to the war. And for many, the current wave of antisemitism is laced with the unmistakable imprint of intergenerational trauma. Psychoanalyst and artist Julia Meyerowitz-Katz describes what it's like to live in this new and not-so-brave world: 'Gradually, antisemitism comes to permeate every area of my life... Wherever I go, I wonder if it is safe. Will I be accepted as a Jew? Should I reveal that I am a Jew?'

The world is burning but, as the great Russian writer Mikhail Bulgakov once wrote, manuscripts don't burn. We want to believe him. In this book, we seek to preserve a historically significant period, to document in real time the profound changes in our private and public lives.

Although a tiny minority group, the Jewish community is not, as sometimes portrayed, a homogenous entity. To reflect this, we gathered a diverse array of contributors: millennials and elders, queer women, women living in regional areas, migrants from the former Soviet Union and Israel, Mizrahi women and women of mixed heritage, descendants of Holocaust survivors and those whose ancestors have lived in Australia for generations. We have stories from artists and lawyers, Jewish educators and cookbook authors, a female rabbi and a socialist Zionist, an Olympic athlete and a professor. The politics of our contributors are as diverse as their backgrounds and their connection to Israel may be fundamental or adjacent to their Jewish identity. There are, however, voices that are not included here – those that deny Palestinians their rights and those that deny Israel's right to exist. That is because both groups are marginal in our community (although some segments of the media and anti-Israel activists like nothing more than to spotlight the latter group as the 'good Jews'). This book is also our attempt to insert our voices in a more representative way – but without reducing the complexity of our identities and affiliations – into the current public vacuum, where Jews don't often speak but are spoken about.

We chose to focus on women's experiences because the sexual barbarism inflicted on our Israeli sisters infiltrated our consciousness and daily lives, invading the intimate moments of our own relationships and pulling many of us onto the streets in protest. Then, many of us have experienced yet another rupture – with our other so-called sisters. 'Where were the strong feminist voices? Why weren't they demanding our girls be released from captivity? Where was the outrage about the desecrated bodies of the Nova festival's young partygoers?' the writer Sharon Sztar laments. She, along with some of the other contributors, raises uncomfortable questions about the state of feminism in Australia, and globally. The indifference of feminist organisations to the sadistic violence perpetrated by Hamas, and the unchallenged captivity of Israeli women, left Jewish women feeling abandoned by the very movements many of them helped build and propel.

The silence about their suffering, as well as other iterations of devastating silence, haunt the pages of this anthology. Otherwise-attentive people don't check in with their Jewish friends and colleagues about their families stranded in wartime Israel nor about their mental health amidst the escalating Jew-hatred in Australia. Fear of cancellation has muffled some, who would otherwise be allies to the Jewish community, from speaking against antisemitism. And Jewish voices that support Israel, even if not uncritically, are often excluded from the public discourse. Unlike other minorities, we are not even allowed to say what is discriminatory against us. 'Nothing much counts as antisemitism anymore for my friends on the left,' observes Mindy Sotiri, social worker and musician. 'Suddenly, people who have never thought about antisemitism are saying, "Stop weaponising antisemitism".'

As Sotiri, along with many other contributors, observes, the rupture is particularly felt in so-called progressive spaces. Spaces where, up until October 7, many Jewish women committed to social justice felt at home. Our youngest contributor, Noa Gomberg, describes feeling unsafe in queer circles: 'I was fifteen and rejected by a community that preached acceptance – the community I had finally summoned the courage to admit I was part of. Where I thought I truly belonged.' She came to feel as if she 'had to choose: the Jewish community or the queer community'.

There is a feeling among contributors that even the language itself has been ruptured. 'The meaning of words I thought I understood is gutted,' writes psychiatrist Lynette Chazan. 'Multiple dizzying inversions are on repeat. Islamist terrorists are freedom fighters. Jewish refugees from Europe and the Middle East returning to their ancestral homeland are colonisers.' We hope that this anthology can become one step towards our reclaiming of the words and concepts currently used against our community.

The world feels ruptured, but as human rights lawyer Melinda Jones, inspired by the kabbalistic concept of *Tikkun Olam* (the drive to repair the world and bring light into the darkness), reminds us – sometimes it is through the cracks that the light gets in. Alongside the angst are stories of resilience, of turning for solace to art, spirituality, and even comedy and cooking. And, in the process, reconnecting to our creativity. Some contributors tell of forging powerful human connections during this troubled time within and outside the Jewish community – encountering the 'kindness of strangers', strengthening existing friendships or reaching out to other people with Middle Eastern origins. For certain writers, their Jewish identity used to be latent, simmering below the surface, but now they are finding themselves at the forefront of trying to repair the world as they engage in advocacy, hit the streets in support of the hostages, and try to rebuild bridges and work towards peace. Whatever we do, many of us are now 'more Jewy', as musician Deborah Conway writes (quoting Bret Stephens), and therefore possibly more whole.

Our hope is that these essays can help us repair the rupture between our community and the world by offering opportunities to hear and understand Jewish experiences. And we also hope that these personal accounts will illuminate something universal – the dangers of misrepresentation and marginalisation of minority groups, and

INTRODUCTION

the corroding effect this can have on individuals, communities and multicultural society. It might be naïve, but maintaining hope is something Jews have always been good at. Running throughout our essays is yet another refrain, a biblical one which has carried our people across the generations – *hineni*, I am here. We are here, our very different contributors seem to be saying in unison. Wounded, but mostly intact.

Lee and Tamar

---

1   Julie Nathan, 'ECAJ Report on Anti-Jewish Incidents in Australia 2024', *Executive Council of Australian Jewry*, 2024.

2   Andrew Tillett, 'One in five Australians is antisemitic: global survey', *Australian Financial Review*, 15 January 2025.

A STONE UNDER HISTORY'S WHEEL

RAMONA KOVAL

I was telling my daughter about an argument at lunch at ours with some Jewish friends whose views differed on a range of issues. One of the couples was still reeling from post-October 7 public and targeted antisemitic attacks on them because they are Zionists. The other couple, public figures too, but more muted in their Jewishness, had claimed it was not legitimate to conflate Jew-hatred in the diaspora with political criticism of Israel, a view that I found unconvincing.

My nine-year-old granddaughter sat between us. What issues, her mother asked me. I was about to say, 'antisemitism in Australia', but I hushed myself and said I'd tell her later. I couldn't bear the idea of having to explain antisemitism to the child. How could I let her know that there are people in the world who would want to eradicate her simply because she had been born into this family, from this mother and this grandmother, and all her Jewish foremothers?

I am now seventy years old.

My parents' generation, the last of the Holocaust survivors that miraculously lived till their nineties and beyond, is dying.

My generation, the children of the survivors, is thinning out too. We are the ones whose parents were in camps, or survived under false identities, or were hidden in wall spaces or in attics. We witnessed the anguish and the damage that haunted the lives of our parents, heard the screams in the dark from their nightmares.

I grew up without grandparents, uncles, aunts or cousins. Both my parents were sole survivors of their families. They tried not to talk about what had happened to them, probably for the same reason I stopped myself around my granddaughter. When I was a child, however, it was hard not to notice my parents' unmitigated sadness, and their barely concealed fear, or the numbers tattooed on the left arms of their friends. All the buried stories and repressed feelings – they kept them down, and I learned by example not to dig them up.

I had avoided Holocaust accounts and the films and the books ever since, at age nine, I was shown the photographs in a publication commemorating the anniversary of the liberation of Auschwitz. My memory of this is linked to the smell of lamb and barley soup we ate that night. It must have been winter for such a hearty meal. I felt like I was going to vomit. My mother asked me when I had begun to feel sick, and I told her it was after Dad had given me the magazine and I had seen a skeletal boy sitting on a metal slide at the opening of a crematorium. Ashes and filth around him and his face a wasted rictus. Why was he smiling, I wondered. Wasn't he about to be inserted alive into the flames?

My mother screamed at Dad that I was too young to see such things. Why did Dad show it to me? To explain perhaps why he was as he was, damaged and broken and anxious?

I found the magazine again in my parents' wardrobe while rifling through the mysteries there, as one does at that age. I should have ended my investigation after trying on my mother's heels and smelling the satin skirt she wore when they were going somewhere special. But I stood on a stool and ventured into a shoebox hidden high up, and I glimpsed the gold-embossed cover and knew exactly what it was. I avoided the wardrobe after that. And thereafter insisted that I couldn't possibly go to sleep in a room with a wardrobe door open. No matter where I was and how old I was, all wardrobe doors had to remain closed, in case the magazine migrated through the years and all kinds of geographies to lie in wait for me.

My avoidance of Holocaust images changed after October 7, when I saw photos and videos taken by the murderous terrorists of their pogrom, of the bodies that had been abused and dismembered and set alight, invoking memories of the crematoria in those photographs long ago. The murders, the rapes, the cruelty – how had this somehow happened again?

The buried images of my nightmares were now in my mind, in the light of day. I felt compelled to revisit the history I had avoided, in the hope of learning something to help me make sense of the present.

I don't have to look through wardrobes now; the online world is one huge forbidden wardrobe of images and history. And so, I give into the ease of searching and one thing leads to another. I see the familiar photos of the crematorium doors with their semicircular shapes. The metal feeding trolleys on which the bodies were placed and shoved into the flames. I can't find the boy on the metal slide.

I do find testimonies, notes and diaries of the Sonderkommandos, the doomed Jewish men who were tasked under threat of death to process other Jews. How they took them to the undressing room, promising that they would be given clean clothes after the disinfecting showers, which were, as we know, gas chambers. And how, after the chamber was sealed and filled with gas, their job was to remove the bodies, shave the hair from the women's corpses, remove the gold teeth from the mouths of the dead, incinerate the bodies, crush any bones left in place, and consign the ashes to pits or the river. Nothing must remain of the crime and Sondercommandos were routinely slaughtered to ensure their future silence. But a few outwitted their tormentors by burying their testimonies, later to be unearthed, in the grounds of the crematorium. And a handful of these men survived too, to tell their stories. For many years after the war, no one wanted to hear what they had to say. It was too horrible to believe.

For three days of reading, I was subdued and sad and dark. When I went to a concert at my granddaughter's Jewish school, while the children sang their lovely Yiddish songs, my head was filled with images of them being rounded up and fed into an industrial killing machine. I couldn't sleep, took sleeping pills three days running. I knew I should stop my search.

But not entirely. I came across the work of Rohkl Auerbach, *Warsaw Testament*, her writing about the Oyneg Shabbos (Joy of Sabbath) group founded by Emanuel Ringelblum in the depths of the Warsaw ghetto. There he gathered a clandestine group of trusted journalists, historians and rabbis to document in real, vivid time the experiences of people in the ghetto.

A writer before the war, Auerbach ran a soup kitchen in the ghetto for writers, artists and performers from Warsaw's vibrant prewar Jewish community. As she fed them and heard their stories, she wrote a series of vignettes to contribute to Ringelblum's archive – an inside account of the moments in people's daily lives, how they lived and feared and loved and faced death.

Her notes joined those collected by other members of the group – thousands of documents and diary entries, photographs and theatre tickets, all evidence of the genocide machine for killing the Jews. Like the testimonies of Sonderkommandos, they were secretly buried so they might be retrieved after the war. Auerbach returned in 1946 to the ghetto to unearth the first cache which had been preserved in buried metal crates and milk churns. The second cache was unearthed in 1950. The third has never been found.

One of the murdered writers, whose words, buried in those crates, outlived her, was the novelist Gustawa Jarecka. Her account of the final deportation of Jews from the ghetto is called *The Last Stage of Resettlement is Death*.

> *One can lose all hopes except the one – that the suffering and destruction of this war will make sense when they are looked at from a distant, historical perspective. From sufferings, unparalleled in history, from bloody tears and bloody sweat, a chronicle of days of hell is being composed, in order that one may understand the historical reasons that shaped the human mind in this fashion and created government systems which made possible the events in our time through which we passed.*

She hoped that her words would hurl 'a stone under history's wheel' to stop a future recurrence of what she witnessed.

I spent the first anniversary of October 7 in the company of family, friends and Jewish community at a commemoration service. It was a solemn day. The venue, a warehouse in an industrial precinct in Moorabbin, selected to foil disruption by angry activists, felt wrong. The location was only disclosed on the day as a security precaution, and there was a massive police presence. I was hiding in my own city. I had already avoided the CBD on Sundays, because it had been captured by loud protesters, marching weekly through the streets, some carrying terror group flags, their faces covered with masks and keffiyehs.

The day before the anniversary, a highly educated and politically left, non-Jewish, old friend who had remained silent for most of the year, emailed to tell me she had been thinking of me but hadn't known what to say. She followed this introductory remark with an account of her new book, her dinner with a mutual acquaintance, and her plans to set off for an overseas holiday.

On her lack of communication over this last year, I replied to say I have been struck by how few of my old friends have thought to check in with me, as the rising tide of antisemitism has made it difficult to feel safe in my city of birth. I tell her I have had to contend with explaining to my grandchildren why their schools need security guards and why people tear down posters of children held hostage by terrorists. I'd asked myself why so many leftists now march with Hamas and Hezbollah supporters? Is this a new thing or have they always supported Islamist terrorism? I say I'm not sure how to interpret the silence, but it feels like abandonment from where I sit. So many dinners, so many years of sharing family and laughter. What did it add up to in the end?

She retorted with sharpness. Insulted by my views of my old leftist associates, she says two things really got to her – my assumptions about people like her, and 'your relentless focus on your experiences of this terrible period'.

Focus on our, meaning Jewish, experiences might seem relentless for her, but it is a long-practiced response of our community to threats from outside. Who else is going to focus and think and write about what is happening to us?

For years I couldn't eat lamb and barley soup. But now I can. And now I can read about the Holocaust and view the photographs, because I understand that I am not a disturbed child anymore. And if we keep these things buried, and refuse to acknowledge what happened, what it was possible for people to do to others, then this terrible knowledge would fade to grey in the world's mind, and it would be as if it never happened, as if people simply made up terrible stories. Already now, the October 7 atrocities are getting buried under the wheels of the Hamas propaganda machine.

The road to the crematoria didn't start suddenly; it was planned and paved for years beforehand, for decades in fact, and I have a hunch that there must have been many people who were not particularly troubled by the antisemitism that they witnessed. Perhaps many, just like my former friend, thought that the Jews were being too sensitive to the remarks, the avoidances, the kinds of events that morph into the corruption of institutions, the creation of regulations, and then the laws that create the hotbed of hatreds that lead to the final destination.

Protecting ourselves from harsh realities doesn't make them go away either. I did not want to sit my granddaughter down and tell her all the ways in which the world might be cruel to her, but she found out anyway. An arson attack on a synagogue a few hundred metres from her school was all over the media and, later that same day, the children were dismissed home early after a man was arrested wielding a hammer in a nearby kosher bakery.

The time has come for us – Jews, non-Jews, all of us who love this country – to open our eyes to the truth of history. To the bloody, bestial, vicious, murderous truth of what can happen when we wilfully ignore the parallels between what is now and what was then.

As Jews, we are often loath to bring up the Holocaust because of politeness, or because it's not happening now, or because we don't want to be that kind of Jew, the noisy kind, the kind that was targeted and tattooed and eliminated. But it would be a mistake to think that the Nazis distinguished between good Jews and bad Jews, sophisticated ones or shtetl ones, Zionists or anti-Zionists. In the end, all the hair was shaved, the gold teeth were pulled and the bodies were burned.

'Never again' means reading and watching and telling and calling out when the first stench of antisemitism reaches our nostrils, not when it has been ignored and played down in the hope that the winds of change will blow it away.

When I was a child, part of me was ashamed of coming from a group of ragtag survivors who had been hardly able to save themselves, much less give me the confidence that they could save me if push came to shove. I had not known the many ways they must have been courageous just to outlive their tormentors.

Since October 7, like many of us, I am strengthened in my Jewishness. After all, there is no hiding place now. We must not bury our manuscripts in metal boxes and milk pails. We must continue to challenge and speak up and write openly. Courage is what I was bequeathed by those who survived. I didn't know it when they were alive, but now I do.

PICKLE PROJECT

ELISE ESTHER HEARST

Pickles, challah, kreplach, a golden slab of frozen chicken soup – a Jewish take on What's in My Bag with a plastic sack of heritage delights. With the phone haphazardly balanced on an olive oil tin, I hit record and plonk these beige Ashkenazi foods on my kitchen counter, following up with a cheeky smile and a 'Shabbat Shalom'. I upload the video to Instagram. Watching it back, I realise I'm wearing a blue and white striped shirt. I have a quick panic about who might read what into that. The colours are, coincidentally, the colours of the Israeli flag. But this is just a video of some food for a Shabbat dinner. How subversive could it be?

It was January 2024. The world had irrevocably changed in the previous three months. My shirt had not been a political choice, rather a sartorial one, yet now there was a part of me daring Instagram's amorphous algorithm: come and get me. I kept the video on my feed.

From a young age I sensed that being Jewish or acknowledging my Jewishness publicly was complicated, and yet I never shied away from it. People's reactions to hearing that I was Jewish amused me:

I've never met a Jew before!
Funny, you don't look Jewish.
What do you mean you don't celebrate Christmas?

I was rebelling against a cautiousness I had been raised with, a warning not to tell others that I was Jewish, lest their response was unkind, or worse. I'd grown up with an atheist grandmother who, having fled from Poland, found religion divisive and loathed being defined by it (despite the fact that most of her friends were Jewish and Shabbat dinners were the highlights of her week). She even liked to tell me how she didn't 'look Jewish'. I never knew what she meant by this. Had she escaped Europe off the back of her button nose?

Then October 7 happened, and for the first time in my life I found myself wondering about the true cost of being Jewish.

Soon after that hellish day I caught the first few whiffs of anti-Jewish racism in Australia. We received instructions from my children's Jewish school not to send them in uniform. A casual clothes day turned into a week and then another, lest someone spot the distinct symbolism on the school emblem and be unkind, or worse...

It did get worse. Each day on the way to school, my children were witnessing violence upon violence: photos of Israeli hostages plastered on light poles being torn down, only to be replaced again, then ripped again – echoes of a war in a land far far away, but also so close to home. The child hostages, Kfir and Ariel Bibas, looked eerily similar to my son, all redheads. How to explain this all to my kids? Oh, you know the story of Purim? Oh, you know the story of Chanukah? Oh, you know how your great-grandmother ran away from Poland? I carried these well-worn tales of persecution in my blood, in my genes, but I had never lived them myself. In a distant land a death toll was rising, and here in my backyard hatred was mounting.

Only a month prior to October 7, I published my debut novel, *One Day We're All Going to Die*, a story of a young Jewish woman in Melbourne grappling with the pressures and expectations of her cultural identity. In November my play, *A Very Jewish Christmas Carol*, inspired by Charles Dickens' famous novella, premiered at Melbourne Theatre Company. A few months later, *Yentl*, an adaptation of Isaac Bashevis Singer's tale which I co-wrote and which celebrates Yiddish culture, was on at the Malthouse Theatre and then again at the Sydney Opera House. Regardless of how openly Jewish I was or wasn't prepared to be, I no longer had the choice to decide for myself. I couldn't wipe my digital footprint. And there was no hiding from the reality that some people didn't like who I was by virtue of my birth. What a pickle.

The first time I put something on my Instagram about *A Very Jewish Christmas Carol*, I was told to free Palestine. I was starting to regret the play's title. Meanwhile, there were hushed discussions about the security of the production, whether this tragicomedy about the power of family and memory was safe to go on at all. The rehearsal room became my refuge; I sidled up to actors huddled around a piano, singing Chanukah songs while the world outside was raging in unimaginable ways with something that, possibly, had been brewing under the surface for decades if not longer.

I knew deep in my *kishkes* that the onslaught of horrors in Gaza depicted in the media would impact the Jewish population in Australia, but I was floored by the extent. Were my book sales impacted? It's hard to say. Did my theatre audiences and actors feel unsafe? Undoubtedly. Had *Yentl*, a multi-award-winning production, suffered from poor attendances and was it likely boycotted? Yes.

All the while, I was cataloguing a personal litany of wounds: feelings of isolation from a progressive arts community I had always felt at home in; appearing on the dreaded 'zio-600' list compiled by doxxers; uncertain career prospects; and a largely silent response from non-Jewish peers and friends to the exponential rise in antisemitism. (But maybe they weren't seeing the same news I was seeing. Maybe their algorithm was different to mine.)

Did my art no longer have a place in this country? Should I make myself less Jewish? Or should I retreat completely? History said: yes. Social media, now a breeding ground for misinformation and extreme levels of antisemitism, definitely said: yes. But my kishkes said: no.

So I began posting videos to Instagram showing what I was eating for Shabbat dinner. I did it as a gentle reminder to my small group of followers that despite a lot of antisemitic content being published online, we (Jews) were still here, doing what we'd always done: existing, and eating. I am here. Here I am. *Hineni*. Now tell me, do you like my matzah balls?

Up to that point I'd mainly used my social media to promote my work, but this was something different – personal, silly, exposing. It felt strange to offer myself up in this way, but by now I felt I'd already lost so much, what did I have left to lose? I needed to reckon with what it meant to be a Jewish artist, and creating these short videos gave me an autonomous vehicle with which to do that.

The response was overwhelmingly positive from Jews and non-Jews alike. What started as a nod to my local Jewish deli became a weekly Shabbat project. Some posts were more earnest, with recipes from my grandmother's kitchen, but most were comical. Each week my content became increasingly ridiculous and more brazenly Jewish. I made a two-minute pickle-tasting video and fast became synonymous with pickles; to this day, friends and followers send me pickle memes and funny pickle-related presents. My post about Caulfield, Melbourne's most densely populated Jewish suburb, where I featured local highlights such as the kosher section of the Hawthorn Road 7-Eleven, the public toilets at Caulfield Park and the house where I lost my virginity, gained over 40,000 views – substantial engagement by my standards.

None of my content was about Israel. This was deliberate. I was not interested in being political. But then, was it perhaps a political act to perform my Jewishness? It was like a social experiment. I waited to see what would happen. *Come and get me…*

When people left hateful comments on my feed, I knew that I hadn't imagined what I had been feeling – a slice of history repeating, echoes from a storied past vividly present. While this realisation was disturbing, at least I felt validated. Plus, for the large part, my content was received with giddiness and gratitude. One Jewish follower wrote to me: 'When I get hateful messages… I am comforted by people like you embracing who you are with no hidden agenda. You're a light in the darkness.'

In the midst of varying shades of grief and loss, I found solace in embracing my identity. My Instagram project connected me to a new audience. I was making people laugh while being unapologetically Jewish. What began as a frivolous rifling through a plastic bag morphed into a testimony of Jewish existence, each post its own little act of defiance. Whether I'd intended it or not, I found that claiming my heritage was indeed a political act. A pickle wasn't just a pickle. Sometimes there is nothing more subversive than being yourself, it turns out.

I AM A JEW

IRENA ZILBERMAN

For Serzhik

It's Saturday October 7. I'm sitting at my mum's dining table. After a busy day, I'm enjoying the relief of being with her and my stepfather, a glass of wine and a home-cooked meal.

We're chatting about which movie we should watch after dinner when my mum's phone rings. It's her friend Valentina; she's on speaker phone, saying something about Israel. Something is happening there. My mum needs to check on Serzhik, her older brother, my uncle, who lives in Ofakim in southern Israel with his wife Vicka. We are used to outbursts of conflict in Israel and have learnt over the years not to take them very seriously. But at the urgency in Valentina's tone, I see my mum's anxiety start to rise. I, too, feel slightly concerned, but also surprised to notice that my main emotion is gratitude. Thank God we live in Australia, I think. Thank God we are safe and not under the constant threat of war.

My mum dials my uncle's number. It rings. And rings, and rings, and rings. A ball of nausea starts forming in the pit of my stomach. Surely not, surely they're ok. My mum tries calling him via Skype, and then Vicka. Still no response. We look at each other, unsure what to do. It's still early in the morning, my mum says, they're probably still asleep.

The next morning, I wake to a text message from my mum, containing one line: *Police have confirmed death.*

That night I go to dinner at my dad's – I don't want to be alone. My dad, his partner and I recount memories of my uncle, a gifted scientist and pianist, a human being who possessed a rare generosity of spirit. I remember how once, when visiting us in Australia, he made potato salad for dinner, with a separate bowl for me without onions, because he knew I hated them. A small gesture, and yet it made me feel so loved.

By now we know that hostages have been taken by Hamas, and that Serzhik and Vicka were shot dead in their home. We manage to find this an absurd silver lining – at least their death was quick and they were not taken hostage. What a relief. But on my way home, all I can think about are their final moments being filled with terror. We don't know any details yet, but my mind is quick to create them. I see my uncle and aunt being awoken abruptly by terrorists storming into their home, my uncle running in his dressing gown towards the front door as a bullet flies into his head.

My uncle had seemed proud of his Jewish identity. He was not particularly observant but he would always send us messages during the holidays, and he chose to continue living in Israel despite the very real possibility of war. I, however, have always felt confused about what it means to be Jewish. Growing up in the 1980s in the Soviet Union, all I knew about being Jewish was that it was undesirable and problematic. A story often told in our house, for example, was how my father was bullied for being Jewish by a kid at school. In retaliation, my father called the kid a fascist, to which the kid replied that it was better to be a fascist than a Jew. My parents gave my brother and me our mother's Ukrainian-sounding surname instead of my father's family name,

Zilberman. And then, my parents managed to move us to Australia, where we thought we would never again have to be scared of being who we are.

In Australia, I went to a Jewish primary school, and although I loved challah bread and enjoyed singing Hebrew songs during various festivals, I didn't understand the meaning of any of the traditions. When I moved to a public high school, I enjoyed socialising with students from diverse backgrounds, and it dawned on me that the world was much bigger than the close-knit Jewish community I had been exposed to until then. At university, I went through a stage of rejecting organised religion after reading Richard Dawkins' *The God Delusion*, and this further fed my confusion. Was being Jewish a religion, culture or an ethnicity? Whatever it was, I hated the intolerance and rigidity I saw in religious practice, like my best friend's family rejecting her partner because he wasn't Jewish. I hated the idea of being 'the chosen people'. What about everyone else?   In my late twenties, I went on a solo trip to Europe, followed by a few weeks in Israel with my father. My experience in Berlin was surprisingly emotional. For me, this city – alive with art, music and nightlife – was a place haunted by ghosts. But Israel didn't stir any powerful emotions in me. It was my first visit, and while I knew of many young people who experienced some sort of spiritual awakening there, it was not like that for me. The cobbled stones and narrow streets of Jerusalem were beautiful, but in my ignorance of their historical significance I remained unaffected. In Tel Aviv, I saw decrepit buildings, dirty laneways and countless hungry street cats; it was a bit of a culture shock.

We stayed with Serzhik and Vicka in Ofakim. The town was small and quiet, surrounded by palm trees and desert. They had a modest house, where my dad sat with my uncle in the kitchen patiently removing pomegranate seeds from their shells, while across the street stood a huge concrete tube – a bomb shelter. I remember finding this confronting. Eventually, we found out that my aunt and uncle were shot from their yard, bullets flying through their windows.

While we are trying to figure out how to process my aunt and uncle's deaths, something else starts happening. We see protests in the news. Well, not protests so much as celebrations. Celebrations of the death of my family and the other innocent people killed, tortured and taken captive. All over the world, people are in the streets celebrating Hamas for their 'just resistance'.

I don't understand. Weren't we the ones attacked and slaughtered? Soon, I start feeling afraid and suspicious of non-Jews. Before I tell a close non-Jewish friend about my uncle, I'm terrified of what her response might be. We've been close for years and I'd never felt scared to share anything with her before. But there is suddenly a lot at stake; her response might determine the future of our relationship. She shows empathy and understanding, but the trepidation I felt lingers and weaves itself into other relationships. Is this the same fear that my parents tried to leave behind?

At work, I tell my colleagues about the murder and they seem supportive, but it's like he passed away from cancer or in some other 'normal' way. 'How awful,' they say. And 'I'm so sorry.' After the first couple of days, it's not brought up again.

One day, I listen to American commentator Ben Shapiro's reaction to the attacks and protests. 'I am a Jew,' he says. 'Those have been the words of the Jewish people for three millennia…Those were the words of Jews in Auschwitz and Treblinka… and those are my words too…' There is grief in his voice, but also a deep rage. Tears start streaming down my face, tears of relief at finally having this emotional mess inside me reflected back. For the first time in my life I can feel it in my body – a spark of my Jewish identity.

In the months that follow the October 7 attacks, I live a double life. I go to work and see my friends; I talk about TV shows and weekend activities. But when I'm alone, I feel despair. In an attempt to feel less impotent, I compulsively listen to podcasts discussing the Israel-Gaza war and the ensuing antisemitism, like *Call Me Back with Dan Senor*, conversations with Douglas Murray and Sam Harris, and I read *The Free Press*. I follow the story of Hersh Goldberg-Polin, a young hostage in Gaza whose mother Rachel is somehow finding the strength to speak and advocate daily for the release of the hostages and for peace. And then, one morning, I open Instagram to see that Hersh and five other hostages have been murdered. On *Call Me Back*, they describe the outpouring of grief in Hersh's neighbourhood in Jerusalem, how hundreds of people stand together in mourning. I wish we'd had an opportunity to communally grieve my uncle, celebrate his life, commemorate how special and loved he was.

For the first time, I feel a deep longing to be in Israel. I remember hearing Michal Cotler-Wunsh say in her speech to the UN: 'The State of Israel does not exist because the Holocaust occurred, it's precisely the opposite. The Holocaust could not have occurred if the State of Israel existed.' Slowly it starts sinking in – what Israel actually signifies to Jews everywhere. I thought the Holocaust was historical trauma, now only contained in books, museums and films. Except now I can see that the trauma never really ended, and that Israel must exist because the persecution, blame and hatred of Jews is continuing, right now, where I live and all over the world. I can never be totally safe in any other country, because whatever it means to be Jewish and however confused I am, I am a Jew.

I know a bit about grief. I work as an intake counsellor with people who have lost a loved one in a road collision. I talk to people about grief on a daily basis. I tell my clients that there is no right or wrong way to experience it, that traumatic grief involves a long period of shock. I encourage them to focus on the small things that help them get through the day. And I know how important the rituals are – the funeral, the sharing of grief, the photos and videos, the small ways the bereaved need to stay connected to their loved ones. I try to remember these things in the days and weeks following my uncle's death. But how do you grieve someone who died thousands of kilometres away? We cannot have a funeral or write a eulogy, we are all floundering, not knowing what to do. My parents decide to create a photo slideshow for family and friends, and I'm relieved there is some tangible thing they can do.

While helping my mum sort photos, I remember that fifteen years ago I recorded some interviews with Serzhik for a documentary I was going to make about my grandparents. I was never able to put the film together, but the material is all there. I pull a dusty plastic container out of my garage, find the recordings. At my mum's house, we watch my uncle tell stories about his life and family. One of his early memories was when, at the age of two, he excitedly opened the gate of their yard and decided to explore the world. He made it two blocks before being caught by a neighbour. His big, joyous smile beams through the screen. Over the coming months, my mum shares the videos with close family and friends, letting me know each time how moved they are to be able to remember him like this. I'm grateful to my 25-year-old self for helping us, in this small way, process our grief.

It's Sunday October 6, 2024, and I'm back at my mum's dining table. There will be more 'protests' all over the world on the first anniversary of the Hamas massacre, while Jewish people mourn. The war is nowhere near the end and more than 100 hostages are still trapped in the tunnels under Gaza. We drink to Serzhik and Vicka. My mum brings out dinner – some grilled fish, vegetables, and potato salad, with a separate bowl for me, without onions.

WE ARE STILL HERE

MINDY SOTIRI

I am reading stories about hostages and avoiding the gaze of my boyfriend. Rach calls from New York and Danni from Barcelona, and I hold the phone close and then far away. Immediate families in Israel are okay. New York is a bubble. Spain is a bust. Danni quietly buys some spray paint. She is tiny and ferocious. My heart is exploding with missing.

I talk on the phone to my mother in New Zealand. She is worried about the Sydney Opera House protest. I am worried about her being the only Jew in the Wairarapa. We're okay, I tell her. We're okay. I look at the way our bodies have woken up, though. Bolt upright. Old fear. Suitcases in the hallway. Familiar as salt.

In the meantime, I don't want much conversation. Specifically, I don't want to talk about the following: water ingress, birthday presents, renovations, real estate, your best friend's mother's dementia, the rain radar, holidays in the Northern Rivers. I am good with limbs and touch.

***

I fly to Melbourne and visit Daniel in hospital. I get him to crack a smile in between the tubes and this feels like a victory. Later my boyfriend and I eat steak and drink wine. High Street in Thornbury. It is quiet outside. I watch the cop cars speed past the restaurant. Just a few extra patrols this evening, they tell us when we walk back to the car. There are federal police standing in a row, arms crossed, lining the street opposite a tiny bar. The sign in the small dark window says *From the River to the Sea*. Muffled beats sound out. Someone steps outside the bar and leans against a wall to smoke a cigarette. All the cops appear dramatic. There is nothing to see. Not really. Just some socialist kids in an inner-north Melbourne bar. Just this stupid wide-awake heart. I am veering between *der chill out* and also *is there any chance I could borrow your attic?* My boyfriend takes my hand. His eyes are on my face. Gentle.

***

In October and November, I sign all the petitions. Jews for a ceasefire. Of course! Why not! Jews against antisemitism. Whoa! I didn't know then how controversial THAT would be. The fear bubbles up inside us, thick and black. My sister says, *Uh-uh. No way. I'm not putting my name on any list.*

Suddenly, somehow, we are whispering in cafes. White women on the internet are getting very angry at Jewish women, who are not at all white, for being too white. Early every morning I edge out of bed, light-headed. Put my hand to the wall. Find my balance. Check the dark sky over Enmore. Jacaranda silhouettes. Frangipani sludge.

***

Danni and Rach and I are chatting via text, remembering when we were teenagers and went camping in the national park. Remembering:

the weird guy who gave us a lift when we hitchhiked from Waterfall Station; the weird park ranger guy who came all the way down from his invisible hut to tell us we couldn't swim nude; the weird guys from the shack along the bay who exchanged food for weed. All those weird guys, we exclaim. It's a miracle we weren't murdered. *All the Weird Guys should be the name of a book*, I say. *Subtitle: Being a young woman*. We are all 50 now. We wear our Magen Davids and say *oy vey* a lot. We plan to meet in Spain.

Jew-hating graffiti appears on the walls in Danni's neighbourhood. She clocks it when out walking with her kid. She waits for dark, then heads back out with her spray can.

My local MP is captured on film saying Jews have tentacles. We infiltrate progressive spaces in the most insidious ways. Huh, I think. Right. Well. She's a lovely woman, mostly. At work I've met with her about prison reform and homelessness and funding for post-release services. Tentacles tucked away for now, I avoid her eyes when I see her in parliament.

I am preparing notes before I see my counsellor. How do I describe what has happened? I turned 50? There was a pogrom? I know I am safe: I dream that I am not. There are businessmen and ferocious German Shepherds. There is a ghost man who hides in cupboards and tries to strangle me. There are many difficult roads and rivers to cross. There are children clinging to their mothers. There are men racing through the streets holding small bodies. This is what I say to my counsellor: *I don't know what is dream and what is inheritance.*

***

Solly's exams finish, and my boys and I go to Ubud for a week. Just me and those babies with their thick, low voices, towering over me.

We float in pools and walk through rice paddies and I focus on their sweetness and try not to check my phone.

On my return, I listen to podcast after podcast, historian after historian. I want to know how the war will end. I want to know how scared to be. Friends with no connection to Israel or Palestine post confident hot takes online. I ask the smartest people I know what to think. The smartest of them have no idea.

I watch the war. There is, of course, no universe in which this makes sense. Women protecting their babies from men's violence. Tanks rolling in. I clock it. Horror at Hamas. Outrage at the Israeli government. Heartbreak for Palestinians. Heartbreak for Jews. And still.

I try to remember the last time I sat out an anti-war protest.

I try to figure out if these *are* anti-war protests or something else.

I call my mother. We crack jokes about potatoes and attics. I make my sister hum along to *Rivers of Babylon*.

My own children, messy-haired, piano-thumping teenagers who have watched too much Scorsese and were never made to sit through Holocaust documentaries, seem okay. I keep checking. Dom says, *I think Zionism has a brand problem*, which I guess is fair enough. Those enormous lucky sweethearts with their long legs and zero fear. They watch it from a distance.

***

My sister and I started celebrating Passover only after we had children. Now I say those prayers like they were always in my bones. Be proud of who you are, my mother says. Be proud. Next year in Jerusalem, we say. Hilarious.

I am in Mparntwe for work. The heat in Alice Springs Correctional Centre soars. In my hotel room I scroll for news online. A cleric in

Western Sydney gives a sermon calling Jews bloodthirsty. Not all Jews, he says. Just most. It is hard to watch. It is hard to not watch. I wonder if this counts as antisemitism.

Nothing much counts as antisemitism anymore for my friends on the left. Suddenly, everybody who has never thought about antisemitism knows how to say *stop weaponising antisemitism*. Everyone is talking about how many friends they have who are Jews (*look at this great bunch of Jews at the protests!*) and how much they love the Jews who hate the idea of Jews having their own homeland.

Unless there are right-wing fascists marching through the streets, we need to be quiet. Mostly, we are told, Jews need to stop complaining. We are told there is a difference between being uncomfortable and being unsafe. *Kvetch kvetch kvetch.*

Hey listen, when you say 'From the river to the sea', I know that you see it as a call to Palestinian liberation, but to lots of Jews it is hard to disconnect this phrase from the call to murder Jews...

SHUT UP BABY KILLER.

Hostage posters are torn down. Private message groups of Jews are shared on social media. Jewish shops are vandalised. Jewish singers are cancelled. Politicians pose next to posters with defaced Stars of David. None of this (we Jews need to understand) is antisemitism. *As if!!* It is something else completely. To suggest otherwise is really just trying to control the narrative for your own nefarious Jewish (*Did I say Jewish? I mean Zionist!*) agenda.

Will we EVER shut up? I wonder.

I think of my grandmother. The numbers etched on her forearm. Her broken toes. Her insistence that some of the Nazis were *really very nice actually*. She has been dead more than twenty years, and I ache and ache wishing she were here. I'm remembering her greeting my sister and me every weekend like we were the greatest thing that ever happened.

***

My sister tells me that you have to put moisturiser on the soft inner parts of the upper arms. Because one day the skin just falls off you. She tells me it happened to our mother in the airport. Just like that. Sudden exposure to air-conditioning. I rub Vaseline Intensive Care on both sides of my upper arms and inspect for signs of collapse. My mother tells me that this ageing thing is a very strange business. *I know*, I say. Sometimes I look in the mirror and think *who is that old lady?* She wants to know where everyone buys their keffiyehs.

My mother also tells me this story. She was at the local chemist and saw a woman who was also wearing a Magen David. My mother approached the woman to say hello, and let her know that she was also Jewish. The woman clutched at her and whispered, *someone spat at me*. And then she rushed off with her medication. This small New Zealand town, where my mother lives, also managed to hound out the recently arrived Israeli family by spray-painting Jew-hate on their fence. My mother tells me the rabbi is coming from Wellington because it turns out there are EIGHT Jews in the Wairarapa. Eight!

***

The sadness of work starts sticking to me in a way I don't recognise. My job is advocating to reduce incarceration; to build ways of responding to harm that don't make things worse. We are not doing so well. There is over-crowding in prisons, and dumb political competitions to see who can be tougher, and children who should never have been locked up dying in cells alone. I want to shut my eyes to all the ugliness. During the day it is prisons. At night it is hostages and executions and the bombing of places where children are sleeping.

When we meet in Spain, Rach, Danni and I take it in turns with the crying. In Palma de Mallorca, the old synagogues that are now churches have been marked with brass plaques. We walk through the squares where, four centuries ago, Jews were rounded up. We sit in nearby outdoor bars in golden Spanish light. We eat fish and drink wine, and in between laughter tell each other stories that we have told each other before, pulling tight on the threads of our history. We FaceTime our parents on the other side of the world and let them exclaim the way parents do when they see their children happy. *Look at you*, they say. *Look at you.*

Danni has been practicing with the spray can. 'We are still here,' she writes. Again and again. 'We are still here.'

THE END OF IGNORANCE

NOA GOMBERG

I can pinpoint the moment I no longer felt safe in the queer community. In the weeks following October 7, I was scrolling through my Instagram reels, pumping my brain with the dopamine my maths homework failed to provide. Until then, my feed had been flooded with messages in support of Israel and the Jewish people; the comments adorned with yellow ribbons. Of course, I also saw Israeli flags being burnt and stickers of Magen Davids inside rubbish bins, but I didn't think much of it. I deduced those people were a misinformed minority, bound to realise that they were supporting terror, not Palestinians. You can call that stupidity on my part. I thought it was hope. For those few weeks, I swam in blissful ignorance. I overindulged in the misguided belief that my generation, Gen Z, had finally realised Israel was not the villain. Unfortunately, ignorance isn't bliss. It's blinding.

I woke up when I saw the inevitable Instagram post caption: 'Queers for Palestine.' A girl with pink hair and glittered eyelids, no older than me, was informing – no, warning – me that as a Zionist, I was unwanted in this community. In a fifteen-second reel, she looked me in the eyes and said, 'If you're a Zionist, you have no place at next year's Pride parade.' And given the overwhelming majority of Jews are Zionists, I took that to mean: I don't care that you're gay. Because of your Jewish identity, you don't belong in the queer community. You are not welcome.

Maybe if I had been a little older or a little tougher, it wouldn't have hurt me as much. But I wasn't. I was fifteen and rejected by a community that preached acceptance – the community I had finally summoned the courage to admit I was part of. Where I thought I truly belonged.

Not long after that, I began to drown in anti-Zionist, and sometimes overtly antisemitic, content. My favourite artists, from queer musicians to actors, attended pro-Palestinian protests where chants praising Hamas and urging the demise of my people proliferated. At my first-ever concert, girl in red punctuated her set with an unprompted 'Free Palestine'. Every single person cheered. I had been listening to her since I was twelve, finding comfort and salvation in her art – just like other queer girls my age. Her iconic song *We Fell in Love in October* made me feel that I would find love. But at that moment, it felt like politics had invaded a space where I was supposed to feel safe; a space where I could just be me, with people like me who loved her music. Instead, two fundamental parts of my biology were being pitted against each other. I had to choose: the Jewish community or the queer community.

Frankly, I'm still not sure why or how the queer community grew so vulnerable to Hamas propaganda – considering they routinely slaughter us in Gaza – or how it has become popular to accessorise keffiyehs with pride pins. I used to be so proud to be part of this community, even when being queer was just in the confines of my thoughts. And now, I'm not sure I want to be associated with it. I'm not any less queer than I was on October 6 2023, but, apparently, there was a secret clause under the terms and conditions of entering this community: 'Warning. May fall victim to clickbait and not research ridiculous claims.'

Most of all, I'm furious. How dare queer influencers deem Israel a 'pinkwashing' state when Tel Aviv has one of the most vibrant Pride parades in the world? How dare they brainwash my generation into thinking being queer has to equal being anti-Zionist? How dare someone say I – a queer woman – don't belong at a Pride parade because of the Magen David around my neck?

Slowly, I began drifting away from queer spaces. Not that I wanted to. I had spent years concealing that part of me – partly out of shame, but mostly because I needed to mature a little more. I wanted to figure out how those feelings sat inside of me, what being gay meant for me. But recently, I was ready to show people who I was. Fully and wholly me. That was up until October 7, when I realised there was a new part of me to hide: my Jewishness. Out of fear.

And I hated that. I should have been welcomed with open arms and rainbow stickers within the queer community. I should have found lifelong friends and unconditional acceptance. But I haven't. It makes no sense that other queer people can bask in the benefits of having a community that loves and accepts them fully, but queer Zionist Jews can't.

***

Since October 7, it hasn't gotten any easier being queer in the Jewish community either. In March 2024, when pro-Palestine protestors attacked the Sydney Gay and Lesbian Mardi Gras, my mum – a loving, well-intentioned woman – said at the dinner table, 'I hope this works as a wake-up call.' The schnitzel felt like rubber between my teeth. The comment seemed to stick to the drywall and stare back at me. When I looked at my mother, mouth agape, she still hadn't processed what she had said or that she'd said it in the presence of her lesbian daughter. In my mind, she had conflated queerness with anti-Zionism. In reality, she just hoped people would see that some 'activists' can be hateful and aggressive, even toward the groups they claim to defend. I understand now where my mother was coming from, and I think most Jews share that sentiment. *I* share that sentiment.

But in this post-October 7 world, I still feel the friction. Sometimes, during my conversations with other Jews, I imagine they expect me to be this angry girl with blue hair, ready to spew anti-Zionist dogma. But I'm not. I won an international public speaking competition talking about my love for Israel, for God's sake! How could I not love a country so full of colour and laughter and chutzpah and, well, love?

***

A few months ago, I was once again seeking comfort in my phone screen when I stumbled across Major Sagi Golan's story. He was only 30 when he was murdered while fighting Hamas terrorists on Kibbutz Be'eri on October 7, just thirteen days before his wedding to a man – Omer Ohana. To me, Sagi, this hero who lost his life protecting other Jewish lives, is the epitome of what it means to be a queer Zionist. Learning more about him – his Jewishness, bravery, kindness, and queerness – made me realise there are other queer Zionists out there. We just need some help finding each other.

And now that I know about Sagi, I realise I can look up 'queer Zionists' on Instagram. I can make Jewish queer friends. Maybe I will even find a Zionist girlfriend! I don't have to be alone anymore. We don't have to be alone anymore.

Thank you, Major Sagi. Your memory is a guiding light.

AGAINST SILENCE

JULIA MEYEROWITZ-KATZ

April 1999, Lithuania. I am standing at the site of one of many pogroms perpetrated by Lithuanians against Jewish people. The silent forested landscape – no birds, no animals, just huge trees and a grassed over burial pit – holds grief, pinning me to the ground. I take photographs, film a video, keep a journal, creating a record of the present while bearing witness to the past. My small acts of protest against the silence, the invisibility. My family fled Lithuania at the turn of the 20th century and those who didn't were murdered in 1941 by their neighbours.

October 7, 2023, Sydney. It takes a few days before I can even begin to tolerate the understanding of what, at first, I could not think was true. I couldn't say the word: pogrom. In 2023, there are still pogroms against Jews.

I am a psychoanalyst, art psychotherapist and artist. In my studio, two days after the pogrom, I plan to continue drawing and painting a series of works that bear witness to my Lithuanian ancestors. I have called the series: *We are still here. And we sing*. But. I can't draw. I can't paint. I am disoriented, flooded with adrenaline. Trying to bear witness to the victims of the past while facing a contemporary massacre seems pointless. Later that day, the evening news shows footage of crowds outside the Opera House. Unrestrained by police, they chant antisemitic slogans and burn the Israeli flag. Glimmers of the rising tide of Jew-hatred.

My acupuncturist tells me that, as with all her Jewish patients, my nervous system is in a frenzy. Similarly, I hear from a physiotherapist who has noticed that the Jewish community is somatically on high alert. She says, 'These bodies are in trauma mode.' I am subsequently diagnosed with two very rare life-changing illnesses. One requiring major surgery, the other, life-long monitoring and treatment. I talk to a health insurance broker who says the number of claims emerging from serious diagnoses amongst his Jewish clientele is unprecedented. Trauma has affected us biologically, making us ill. This is how some epigenetic changes occur.

Following weeks of feeling lost and unsettled, I find, in a corner of my studio, a large unstretched, unprimed canvas – almost 200 x 200 cm. I lay it on the floor; it is four times bigger than the largest size I usually work on. I prime it with transparent gesso. Moving around the canvas while spreading the gesso, I realise that it has become a container; it has edges, a border, it feels safe. The gesso does not hide the colour of the raw canvas, every mark I make must be a commitment.

I decide to use the canvas both as an environment on which to draw and paint – I can crawl or walk on it and leave traces of my movement – and as a vertical image that hangs on the wall like a traditional painting. Gesso greedily grabs the paint and is unforgiving; it tears my skin open. While moving between floor and easel, as I crawl around the canvas, or brush my hands over it, I must be cautious. This creates a tension between wanting to get lost in the process and being forced to remain very aware. This process, like the life I am currently living, hurts. I deliberately use a restricted palette and marks that evoke life-size suggestions of body through lines, drips and brushstrokes.

Because of the painting's size, and my slow recovery from surgery, it takes months to complete it. The painting becomes a reassuring presence in my studio, giving me a sense of continuity. The sight of it offers me a record of living through an existentially critical period which has sapped me of my emotional and physical reserves. My body is reaffirmed by this concrete evidence of my art-making capacity.

In later weeks, the tide of antisemitism rises. Protestors wave flags that carry clear symbols of genocide against Jews. The red triangle – a swastika for the 21st century. Approximately 600 of us in a Jewish WhatsApp support group for creatives and academics are doxxed. I didn't know what doxxing meant until it happened to me. Like many Jews in Europe during World War II, I am on a list. Just as I cannot remove myself from the list, I cannot stop people defacing posters of the hostages in the area where I live. Gradually, antisemitism comes to permeate every area of my life. Hamas may have invaded Israel, but diaspora Jews are all psycho-somatically invaded. Most nights, I dream of being trapped in dark tunnels. I wake up at 3.30am gasping for breath. Resolved to find my way back to some kind of normality, I spend time in my studio whenever I can.

I find I am hyper-aware of being Jewish. Wherever I go, I wonder if it is safe. Will I be accepted as a Jew? Should I reveal that I am a Jew? I am told by another resident artist in my studio that 'Jews have all the power.' I manage to say: 'How can that be? We are one of the smallest minority groups in the world. And in Australia, there are only around 100,000 of us.' That relationship has never recovered from this exchange. Now, even my studio feels unsafe.

In my work as a psychoanalyst, I assume I will carry on as usual. I have navigated challenging personal issues with my clinical mind intact before. I assume I will do it again. But. The clinical floor on which I used to stand has vanished. My job is to understand unconscious communications, to process emotional experience. To sink into reverie and find the imagery that will help my patients to understand themselves better. But when I am with a Jewish patient, we are both drowning in sorrow.[1] She says, 'At least now we know. They hate us.' The white noise of anxiety is loud. I say: 'Today we can't think, we can just be.' Nothing has prepared me for this, for facing the loss of personal and communal safety, the existential threats that we thought belonged to previous generations, together with my Jewish patients.

I am with another, non-Jewish, patient, fumbling to find my clinical mind. He describes watching a graphic video of a wailing mother holding her limp dead baby in Gaza. Then, turning his head and looking at me intently, he says, out of the blue, that he doesn't know who to trust. In an environment where unconscious processes are privileged, it occurs to me that perhaps, aware that I am Jewish, he doesn't know if he can trust me. He might be unconsciously frightened that his trusted therapist is a Jewish baby-killer, as antisemitic tropes would have it. Absorbing and working with unconscious fears is part of my job, but what do I do when my patient's fear is about my being Jewish, in the context of increasing antisemitism? I tell myself to breathe. It takes some time before I can recover enough so that we can have a conversation about this.

As psychoanalytic psychotherapists and patients know, there is value in shared, contemplative silence. The consulting room is often quiet while the work of deeply generative thinking takes place. But there is a darker side to silence. Over the last year, I have come to understand how profoundly silence can 'other', particularly in the professional community in which I have been deeply engaged for decades. Such 'othering' silence enables hatred to grow unseen and unnamed. It makes me feel isolated, amplifying my experience of living, as a Jew, a parallel life.

Two months after the pogrom, two colleagues and I offer to present our experience as Jews since October 7 to a small, closed group of analysts. We are apprehensive but feel compelled to break the silence. And then we are overwhelmed by the number of attendees and the support we receive. The support from members of this group turns out to be an anomaly in my professional milieu; generally, so many colleagues are silent. Or unconsciously, or even overtly, hostile.

Soon after, a Jewish colleague and I are asked to draft a position statement about the war for a professional body that has issued other position statements in the past. We to-and-fro with them in an effort to find a position with which everyone is comfortable. Despite the clear empathy in our draft for all innocents affected by the war, the committee cannot agree with us calling out Hamas as brutal terrorists. They fear alienating Muslim patients. Gaslighting Jewish colleagues and patients doesn't seem to matter. Despondent, we withdraw our statement. The response to our withdrawal is – silence.

The silence continues when I attend a prominent annual professional conference. Nervously, but determinedly, I out myself as a Jew, wearing my Magen David and my yellow pin in honor of the hostages. Of all the delegates, many of whom I have known and worked alongside for years, only one non-Jewish colleague approaches me. She gently touches my arm, and says, 'I think of you all, I feel for you all.' Motioning to my yellow pin, she says, 'Good for you. I wish I'd worn mine.' I hold back tears.

I receive a call for papers from a different psychotherapy body where my work has been well-received several times over the decades. I send an abstract. It is about my experience as a Jewish clinician. They turn me down; the committee feels that the Jewish experience would be 'too sensitive'. The person delegated to convey this news tells me there are shops in her suburb in Sydney that have 'No Jews' signs.

Another conference. A non-Jewish colleague approaches me: 'How is your health? I have heard you have been unwell.' An ordinary question in ordinary times. But these are not ordinary times for Jews. I don't know what to say. I am thinking: unwell? Seriously? For almost a year there has been a war against Jews. Where have you been?

In all of this, on the Rosh Hashanah of this terrible year, one of my non-Jewish colleagues sends me a text message: 'Dear Julia, I am thinking of you on Rosh Hashanah and sending good thoughts to you… at this unbelievably difficult time.' I am not counting, but because there has only been one, I can't help but notice it and so I count. And I am grateful. I appreciate, too, the heartfelt messages of support from a handful of colleagues on the one-year anniversary of October 7.

I keep returning to my studio. I keep working on the painting. It becomes more layered. As I paint, my thoughts move between the silent trees of Lithuania and the grassed over burial pits to the devastation of October 7 – burnt corpses, burnt homes, burnt cars, pools of blood. Still, I keep painting. What began as an act of containment and survival, is now an act of defiance. Against hatred. Against illness. Against the ongoing tides of antisemitism and the accompanying silence.

Finally, the painting is done. It now hangs on the wall along with other artworks in my studio. After a while, I tentatively begin working on several new smaller paintings. I am not sure yet what they will become, but I am painting. Bruised and battered, and with a permanent heartache, but I am still here.

---

1   Clinical material draws on the emotional truth of my clinical experience, but the specific details have been altered to protect confidentiality.

NANA'S BRACELET

JEMIMA MONTAG

I'm just like Nana was in many ways: hardworking, dedicated to family and passionate about feeding people. But there is a part of her I never imagined I would share: the fear she experienced as a young girl afraid to show her identity. Following the harrowing events of October 7, as I prepared to represent Australia at the Paris 2024 Olympic Games, I found myself questioning whether to conceal my Jewish identity. This feeling was an eerie reminder of Nana's internal conflict in Kraków in 1939. As the Olympic Games grew nearer, I stood in front of microphones, on start lines and in airports, hyper-aware of my safety as a Jewish athlete. This duality of fear and pride dominated my year.

Nana spoke very little of her memories of the Holocaust, but she left behind pages of handwritten notes. Within these pages I discovered the bond she shared with her sister Ruth, which was crucial to her survival. In Auschwitz, Ruth was resourceful and optimistic. If there was a job to be done, she was quick to volunteer. She took calculated risks and knew when to stay in line. By mid-January 1945, the sisters were sent on the Death March to Ravensbrük. They took the cloth band from their striped frocks and tied their wrists together. They'd stay united, dead or alive.

Despite the Nazis' intentions for her, Nana lived 94 years. Before she passed, my aunt had Nana's gold necklace cut into three identical bracelets for my sisters and I. They are yellow gold and chain-like, with a certain old-worldly charm. Mine gives me strength, a constant reminder of her resilience. I could feel the bracelet moving up and down my forearm as I competed at my first Olympic Games, in Tokyo in 2021, just weeks after Nana passed. Crossing the finish line, I pointed up to her in the sky, acutely aware that I would not have had this opportunity if it weren't for her will to survive.

In 2022 and 2023 I competed at the World Championships in Oregon and Budapest, and the Commonwealth Games in Birmingham. At the finish line of each race, journalists were intrigued by the story of Nana's bracelet. I explained that when I feel it moving during a race, I am reminded of her sacrifice and unwavering determination. Because of her, I now have the privilege of pursuing my sporting dreams, however challenging they may seem in the moment. I also feel bound to my sisters, each with her identical bracelet – a reminder of how the bond of family can help us endure the unimaginable. During these post-race interviews, I felt proud to share Nana's survival story with millions around the world.

The following year things felt different. After October 7, I worried about what could happen if my Jewish identity featured prominently in the public eye. I began to question whether my mental health and personal safety would be at risk if I continued to speak to the media about Nana. I was preparing to represent our country at the Olympic Games in Paris, the very city where Nana sought refuge after the Holocaust, and had hoped it would be a symbolic and memorable celebration. But when various Jewish sporting social media pages tagged me as a Jewish athlete to look out for at the Paris Games,

Mum prompted me to remove the tags. It did not feel safe for the world to know that I was Jewish in the lead up to the biggest global sporting event on the calendar. Removing my name from these posts felt safe yet disappointing. I wished to demonstrate my pride of and connection to our community, but felt that I had no choice but to hide.

By May 2024, I had made an active decision to conceal my Jewish identity to protect my safety and mental health ahead of the Olympics. My training partners and I landed in Warsaw for a competition, and having never been to Poland – my grandmother's birthplace – I was curious about how I'd feel there. I spent the day prior to the race walking through the old town, revelling in memories of my grandparents – pickles, pianos, goulash and crepes. As the sun set, I wandered into a Chopin piano recital and was welcomed with a slice of poppyseed cake. A little old lady sitting alone gestured for me to sit beside her. We didn't utter a word for the duration of the concert. Seeing only the outline of her figure and her delicate hands from the corner of my eye, I imagined that she could be Nana. In that moment, my fear dissipated and I felt my Jewishness deeply, with no ambivalence. But the feeling didn't last long.

As the Olympic Games approached, I grew more on edge. I kept thinking of the 1972 Munich Olympic Games, at which eleven members of the Israeli team were murdered by Black September terrorists. I was set to compete in the 20-kilometre race-walk and the mixed marathon race-walk relay, both in open public spaces with unprotected exposure.

The day of my first competition, I was focused on executing a plan. We awoke early to a thunderstorm. High humidity and a 30-minute race delay followed. Soon we were ushered to the start line – 48 of the best female racewalkers in the world filled with nervous excitement. The Eiffel Tower was only a stone's throw away and yet I hardly noticed it, distracted by the bellowing noise of 30,000 fans on the sidelines. Like a pack of warriors, we marched around the one kilometre loop for one and a half hours. At the beginning, it felt like complete sensory overload. I could see my biggest rivals beside me, I could hear the crowd screaming for their countrywomen, and I could feel the humid air and the weight of expectation upon my shoulders. Eventually, fatigue set in, and I questioned my desire for a medal. I found myself in fifth position when my sister's voice cut through the noise of the crowd. 'This is your race!' she shouted, reminding me not to let this opportunity drift away. I was able to use my family and support team's energy as the motivation to overtake two athletes, and eventually crossed the finish line in third place.

Six days later, I became the first Australian woman in over 50 years to win two medals in Athletics at one Olympics. Journalists asked me about Nana's bracelet once again. I felt conflicted. I wanted to say something meaningful for the Jewish community, to speak out against antisemitism, particularly in a year like 2024. But another part of me wished to stay quiet. I ended up giving vague answers, speaking about the importance of family and how excited I was to have them on the sidelines, skipping the details of Nana's life that I had previously felt so proud to share publicly.

In some ways, the choice to conceal my Jewish identity this year has made me feel disappointed in myself. Reflecting on this feeling, I asked Dad whether Nana was cautious with her Jewish identity after the Holocaust and he confirmed that she was. If asked about her Auschwitz tattoo, she would say it was a boyfriend's phone number. However, with this degree of caution, she was able to build a new life with a home that was a celebration of Polish food, Jewish rituals, Parisian fashion and music. The door was always open and no one could resist Nana's cakes. While I do not know when my fear will diminish, I hope that I can feel safe enough to speak about Nana's bracelet again soon.

THE PRIVILEGE OF BEING A PACIFIST

JOANNE FEDLER

I had never touched a gun until one was placed in my hands by a man I trust, an accomplished marksman with a military background. He's not Jewish, but he loves Jews, for reasons that remain unclear to me. I see him for health reasons because shooting is not his day job. He's eased me from physical pain on countless occasions. He fits me in when his schedule is full. He makes me feel safe.

It was weeks after October 7, and while I was lying, face down, on his massage table, we spoke about the horrors committed by Hamas and Israel's retaliatory bombing of Gaza. For some time now, I'd barely slept, jolted awake by intrusive images of a pregnant belly sliced open. A child's foot severed. A baby, *godhelpus*, in an oven. Shock and exhaustion were lodged like shrapnel in my neck and back muscles

I asked him, given his army background, to explain Israel's military strategy in Gaza in response to the terrorism we'd just witnessed. I was deeply troubled by aspects of it. 'What about those caught in the crossfire? How many innocent people will die?'

'Many. This is war.'

'But I'm a pacifist,' I whimpered.

'If they came for your children, you wouldn't be.'

Tears dammed in my throat. 'I'm scared.'

He was quiet for a while, letting me cry.

'I have an idea, but it's a bit out there.'

And that is how I came to be holding a gun (without bullets), which he took from his safe and placed in my hands.

'Envisage protecting yourself and your family.'

I closed my eyes. The metal was heavy, icy cold in my palms. I wondered if this is what safety feels like, to be in possession of an instrument of murder like Artemis, the Greek goddess of the hunt, protector of women and children, who carried a bow and arrow to stop those who would hurt the innocent and vulnerable.

I tried to imagine in what version of myself I could ever pull a trigger.

***

When he was a child, I forbade my son from playing with toy guns. I wouldn't have them in our home. And he was the only kid who wasn't allowed Call of Duty when all his peers were blowing each other up online.

'This is a non-violent household,' I told him.

'I'll still play it when I'm at my friends',' he heckled.

'I can't monitor what you do when I'm not around. But under this roof, these are the rules. Violence is real, it hurts real people.'

I was unwavering on few principles as I blundered my way through parenting, but 'guns are not toys' was one of them, even if I copped a lot of abuse from my son over the years for my stubbornness.

In June 2014, three Israeli teenagers, Eyal Yifrach, Gilad

Shaer and Naftali Fraenkel, were abducted in the West Bank while hitchhiking. On the mantlepiece in our loungeroom, we kept candles lit alongside their photos and prayed for their safe return. Those boys were not much older than my own children. When the news came that their bodies had been found in a shallow grave, I was inconsolable. As my son hugged me, he whispered, 'I won't play Call of Duty anymore, Mum.'

Before I moved to Australia, I spent my early lawyering years as a women's rights advocate, fighting sexual and domestic abuse in South Africa just as the country was shaking off Apartheid and becoming a democracy. In my late twenties, a hungry and passionate warrior for justice, I served on a commission to draft new domestic violence legislation. I trained police, prosecutors and magistrates to recognise their unconscious racism and sexism. Back then, I believed education and legal reform was all it would take to make the world safer for women and children. But in the years after Nelson Mandela was released, despite our Anti-Violence Against Women movement's best intentions and carefully targeted legal strategies, we were bludgeoned with failures. We encouraged women to leave abusive relationships because the 'law would protect them', not foreseeing the danger of 'separation assault' which is often lethal. Statistics of rape and domestic violence soared, as did femicide.

I defended several women who had killed their abusers, but it was difficult to persuade judges of the danger posed by a man asleep or with his back turned, and so we often struggled to prove they'd acted in legally recognised 'self-defence.' They escaped their violent relationships only to be convicted of murder.

During my last decade in South Africa, six people I knew were murdered, dozens raped, hijacked and held at gunpoint. It took the gang rape of someone dearly beloved to me, for me and my partner to rip our small children from the bosom of grandparents and cousins and immigrate to Australia, a place far from the rampant random lawlessness of my homeland. I arrived in my new country with my faith in advocacy to 'end violence against women' crushed. It was as foolish as trying to 'end the patriarchy'.

But still, I clung to the ideal of a non-violent world. I was a pacifist, after all...

***

Months after October 7, I travelled to Singapore to train with complexity thinker and educator, Nora Bateson. I was spurred to learn from her after I read her article 'Communication is Sacred,' in which she writes about the damage caused by misrepresentation.[1] I was emotionally shaken and bruised after a WhatsApp group of Jewish Australian Creatives and Academics I belonged to was doxxed and vilified, with our photographs and personal information circulating on social media. Some members were threatened and had their homes and businesses violated.

I needed a new way of thinking – not just about the impact of the doxxing on me personally, but my relationship to violence in the post October 7 world. As an activist, I had always assumed that all social problems could be fixed if only the correct 'solution could be found and enforced'. But now, I could see no resolution.

With Nora's guidance, I understood why direct correctives don't repair what we call 'wicked problems' which are intractable social issues, ambiguous and impossible to solve. More so, direct correctives often trigger unintended negative consequences; because everything in a complex system is interconnected, nothing can be lifted out of context and fixed without disturbing the entire system. Violence is one such wicked problem. It is often a symptom of what has been submerged and hidden over time. Without addressing these unseen forces, violence will just keep reappearing in different guises and places. As a pacifist, I had always externalised violence. It was 'out there' – I was above it, morally and ideologically. How could I miss it? The obvious splitting off that happens when we disown what we find personally repugnant.

But Tyson Yunkaporta, the Indigenous scholar and author, says: 'violence itself is part of the system, whether you like it or not, and needs to be distributed throughout it.'[2] If you're a pacifist, he asks, *to whom are you outsourcing your violence?*

Recently, this question stopped me in my self-righteous tracks.

***

'War,' Virginia Woolf wrote in *Three Guineas*, 'is a man's game. The killing machine has a gender and it is male.'

I often fantasise we might do better with female leadership, but I doubt we'll ever know. In the world we inhabit, war is part of the toxic masculine culture and problem-solving that has been gamified in Call of Duty and other soul-disfiguring forms of teenage 'entertainment.' Terrorism and state sponsored aggression are mottled into the fabric of our lives like dirty dollars and drugs. Our moral aversions do not dissolve or nullify them. The prisons and terror cells are the shadowlands of our cities and they are our responsibility even if we, ensconced in our peaceful suburbs, never see them. The job of the adult, Carl Jung pointed out, is to identify and integrate the shadow, not just individually, but collectively.

In the months after October 7, I waited for my previous comrades with whom I'd fought against sexism and racism to condemn the murders and sexual violence committed by Hamas. Surely they'd call for the return of the hostages and express outrage at the violation of Israeli women. Instead, they only denounced Israel's aggression and applauded South Africa's case in the ICJ, headed by a professor who had taught me International Law. His was the only class I ever walked out of, in tears, unable to articulate that what I had just been subjected to was the violence of antisemitism, dressed in legalese.

I began to see the toxic fascism in parts of the left, my once-political home; its performative selective outrage masquerading as 'anti-Zionist pacifism'; the Jew-hate, finally aired. There was something of a relief to it – to see it stripped bare, the irrational antipathy towards Jewish people that my father had warned me about, which I'd pooh-poohed, because the Holocaust was like, so 1939.

I tried, at first, to engage with a few friends who, I hoped, could hold a non-binary position, or at least admit to the complexities of this age-old Israeli-Palestinian conflict which was anything but simple. At some point, rage overtook my fear, and so began the great unfriending and blocking on social media. It was self-care. I had to arrest the thousand daily assaults on my nervous system as I just couldn't take another smug, ill-informed post about the Israel-Hamas war. Each extinguishment gave me the only sense of power I had left. Perhaps this too is a kind of violence – deleting opinions we don't want to hear. I joined online Jewish groups that had the word 'peace' in them, but found it jarring to be amongst a cohort of anti-Zionist Jews who focus only on condemning Israel in this climate of existential peril, as if peace is something one side in a struggle can achieve alone.

As I witnessed others' self-righteous, easy pacifist opinions about struggles in which they had no skin, I wondered whether my own pacifism would survive a pressure test – not as a thought experiment but in real life. *If they came for your children…*

***

In her essay 'Regarding the Pain of Others', Susan Sontag wrote: 'Someone who is perennially surprised that depravity exists, who continues to feel disillusioned (even incredulous) when confronted with evidence of what humans are capable of inflicting in the way of gruesome, hands-on cruelties upon other humans, has not reached moral or psychological adulthood. No-one, after a certain age, has the right to this kind of innocence, of superficiality, to this degree of ignorance or amnesia.'

October 7 was the breaking of a spell and the initiation into a maturity I hoped I could evade with enough magical thinking. My idealism about 'peace' is gone – it died with Vivian Silver[3] and those young dancers at the Nova festival. As a Jew, I cannot afford the naivete and toxic positivity of believing meditation and prayer are enough for us all to live happily ever after from the river to the sea. It's disrespectful to the dead to be that tone-deaf to the violence by which they perished.

Still, each morning, as I hold onto my hostage tag, I find myself praying that they are still, *please please God*, still alive. I ask for protection for the young men fighting on all fronts, knowing that if my children had been taken hostage, soldiers like Arnon Zmora would give their lives to bring them home.

I find it tough to look at social media feeds showing the ruined lives of the civilians in Gaza. My heart aches for all the human suffering unleashed by war. I used to be the first to call out injustice and bear the brunt of speaking the truth. But I don't know any more what is true and so I am mute. At times, it has felt like a failure of courage and conviction.

But now, with compassion towards my own shadow, I understand it as the silencing caused by a double-bind. Sometimes, despite our loftiest intentions, there is no way to behave in alignment with our deepest values because those values have never been stress-tested.

Still, through the haze of this confusion and trauma, some clarity is emerging as I come to a sorrowful reckoning with evil and the limits of liberal ideas of pacifism: I will no longer engage in intellectual debates about 'non-violence' with people who have no persecution, slavery or concentration camps in their history.

To be a pacifist, it seems to me, is a privilege for those who have never feared for their survival.

As for me, I've held a gun now. So maybe I, too, in a moment of fear or error, am capable of terrible things. Even Artemis, the guardian of the weak and vulnerable, on occasion, committed unforgivable acts against the innocent. And isn't she the one you'd want on your side if they came for your children?

---

1   Nora Bateson, 'Communication is Sacred', *Kainos* [Substack], 6 February 2024, beiner.substack.com/p/communication-is-sacred-by-nora-bateson.

2   Tyson Yunkaporta, interview by Jamie Wheal, *Collective Insights* [podcast], 5 October 2021.

3   Vivian Silver, a lifelong peace activist and co-founder of Women Wage Peace, was murdered in the Kibbutz Be'eri massacre on October 7.

WHAT HURTS MORE?

KERRI SACKVILLE

As a Jewish day school student in the 70s and 80s, I was a bit of a rarity. Nearly every other kid in my year at Moriah College had either been born overseas, or was the child or grandchild of immigrants. Not me. Three out of my four grandparents were born in Australia, and the fourth, my Nana Mim, emigrated as a child from Poland. I was third-generation Aussie on three sides of the family, and this made me feel special. I belonged in this country. I felt grounded in a way I suspected many of my classmates did not.

My school friends had parents and grandparents with Eastern European accents. They had lived through unspeakable horrors of the Shoah before escaping to this country. My connection to the Holocaust was far more distant. My grandparents spoke with broad Aussie accents. Nana Mim left Poland well before the war through an accident of fate. Her Uncle Itch had moved to Australia in the 1920s and sent for his sister Edie, but when she declined, his other sister, Sara – Mim's mother – joined him with her family. Edie and her family were eventually murdered by the Nazis.

I knew the story, but it felt remote. I did not feel touched by the intergenerational trauma that informed so many of my friends' lives.

Still, I was haunted by the Holocaust. One night, lying in bed in my very Aussie bedroom, with its green shag pile carpet and wrought iron bed, I performed a thought experiment. I closed my eyes and forced myself to imagine the Nazis at our front door. I visualised them dragging my parents away, throwing me in a truck, pulling my sister by her hair. It was horrible. I pushed the thoughts out of my mind. I returned to my Judy Blume novel.

Life was safe in Australia. I felt secure. I never experienced even a whiff of antisemitism, mostly because I never left my Jewish bubble. My friends were Jewish. My parents' friends were mostly Jewish. We lived in the eastern suburbs of Sydney, down the road from Zabar's Deli. If there was antisemitism in the country, I was blissfully unaware.

Even when I did venture out of my bubble, I didn't encounter bigotry. If anything, I was met with mild confusion. At fifteen, I won a major role in a TV mini-series and spent three months on set with the cast and crew. They all knew I was Jewish (because I'm chatty, and I told them), but they weren't quite sure what that actually meant.

'So you're from Israel?' one of the actors asked.

'No,' I said and started to clarify, but he had already lost interest.

I realised then what would become glaringly clear in adulthood: I had been incredibly sheltered at Moriah. Out in the world, I felt a pervasive sense of being different, of not quite fitting in. I didn't experience any negativity directed at me, but I certainly experienced ignorance and indifference. I was always keen to explain my culture ('No, we don't celebrate Christmas.' 'No, we don't believe that Christ is our saviour.' 'No, we don't speak Hebrew at home!'), but few people ever asked.

There was only one 'incident', as I thought of it, back in the mid-1990s. I was having a blood test and the nurse, struggling to get a vein, muttered: 'You're a bit of a Jew with your blood!' I froze, stunned into silence by her words.

In later years, I married a Jewish man, had Jewish kids and forged a career in the media. I never became famous, but I had a public profile and felt a responsibility from the earliest days to be open about my culture. I wrote often about being Jewish in my columns and social media posts, spoke about it in interviews, and referenced my Jewishness in all my books. It takes a thick skin to survive as a female in the media, and I experienced all kinds of sexism and misogyny, but I never experienced hatred for being a Jew.

After October 7, that all changed.

***

I learned about the massacre from a friend with family in Israel. She told me that three of her niece's friends were killed at the Nova music festival.

'Three of her friends?' I repeated, shaking my head. I couldn't make sense of what she was saying. 'What do you mean?'

It took me several hours to process the magnitude of what had happened. These beautiful young people, these children, these men and women – slaughtered, kidnapped, held in Gaza. My mind struggled to hold the shape of the horror. I imagined my son at the music festival. I imagined my daughter. I cried, on and off, for two days. These were all of our children. These were all of our friends. I felt the foundations of my world shift.

Soon after, I was granted permission to write a newspaper column about October 7. I wrote about my fear of antisemitism in Australia since the attacks and my devastation at the loss of life on both sides. My aim was to diffuse tensions, to increase understanding and bolster empathy for my fellow Jews. The article was warmly received. I was grateful to have a public platform.

My birthday is October 17. I was not in the mood to celebrate. My Jewish friends offered me muted birthday wishes. My non-Jewish friends offered their regular, cheery greetings.

Are you doing something fun to celebrate? one asked in a group chat. There were four of us there and I was the sole Jewish person.

No, I typed back. *I'm not in the mood. I've been incredibly upset about what is happening in the Middle East.*

The chat went quiet for several minutes. Finally, a different member of the chat replied: *The world is crazy!*

That was it. No words of sympathy or some sort of recognition. Since my birthday, I've heard nothing from two of those friends. The third made plans with me twice and cancelled both times. All three are now gone. Completely out of my life.

***

What hurts more, the silence of erstwhile friends, or the open hostility of strangers?

The media turned. Social media turned. Several prominent 'influencers' – many of whom call themselves 'feminists' – posted aggressive anti-Zionist rants online. These were the progressive left, people I had admired and supported in the past. It was profoundly shocking. I felt violated. I can tolerate differences of opinion – I mean, I trade in opinion pieces – but this was blatant misinformation. Many of these influencers called Israeli Jews 'colonisers', erasing our ancient ties to the land of Israel.

One by one, several of my non-Jewish friends in the media joined the chorus, making their own antisemitism blatantly clear. They 'liked' offensive posts or wrote inflammatory posts of their own. Some thinly disguised their antisemitism as anti-Zionism. Others didn't bother hiding their contempt for us. *Stop using the Holocaust as an excuse. Go back to Poland. Good on Hamas. It was resistance! There were no rapes.* This wasn't empathy for the Palestinians. This was hatred of the Jews. It shattered me, because these people knew me, the Jew. We used to share coffees, meals, our life stories, secrets. How could I not have known what they thought about me and my people?

I have been writing opinion pieces for over twenty years. I am told I am good at it. Sometimes I can change people's minds with my words. So I tried to use my platform for good. *There are two peoples who are indigenous to the land of Israel*, I posted on social media. *This is the source of the conflict.* I was measured. I was calm. I knew that I would be able to help people see that Jews could care deeply about the hostages and their dead, and also feel devastated at the loss of Palestinian life.

I was wrong. The comments were fast to arrive, the likes of ZIONISTS LOVE GENOCIDE.

I've had vile comments in the past, sure, but I've usually been able to disarm the commenter with humour. More than once, I've turned a troll into a fan.

Not this time.

Initially, I responded as gently and reasonably as I could. I sent links to articles, explaining the history of the Jews in Israel. ZIONIST PROPAGANDA, they wrote back. STOP MAKING EXCUSES FOR COLONISERS.

No argument worked. Nothing could make the commenters reflect on their own prejudices. Why did they care so passionately about this one conflict, but not about the ones in Yemen or Sudan? Why did they care about the suffering of other minorities, but dismissed – even mocked – the suffering of Jews? Why did they 'believe all women' except Jewish women?

No argument worked, I realised, because antisemitism is not logical. You can't use reason to dismantle hate.

With that dawning realisation, something happened to my brain. A sense of hopelessness and impotence overwhelmed me and, in the vacuum it created, the horrors of the Holocaust finally caught up with me, flooding my consciousness, running on a continuous loop in the background. My body was in Sydney, but my mind now was in the *shtetls*. I saw the trucks rolling in, saw the trains, the piles of bodies, saw my father shot, heard my kids screaming for help. The intergenerational trauma I believed I'd been free of had been there all along, lying dormant inside me.

It was the closest I have ever come to a mental breakdown. I cried and I shook, and at night I lay sleepless. I could not talk myself down. For several weeks, I felt constantly frightened and constantly on alert.

In desperation, I went to my GP and got a script for antidepressants; the first time I had taken them in many years. I cut down on my news intake, limited my social media and disengaged from conversations about the Middle East. I rewatched movies from the 1980s, a time when I still felt completely safe. It took three or four weeks for the fear to recede and the Holocaust visions to fade.

Eventually, I felt ready to write about my experience. I also wanted to write about the doxxing of over 600 Jewish creatives and academics, which happened around the time of my crisis and made the news. I pitched the idea to the editor of my column, several times. I even offered to waive my fee. I literally begged for the opportunity. I was firmly told 'no', they weren't interested in my take. They'd heard enough on the topic. No one reads those pieces anyway. They did, however, eventually run an article by another Jewish columnist, calling for the end of Israel as a Jewish state and blaming antisemitism in the diaspora on Israel. She, an anti-

Zionist, was allowed to write her opinion on matters related to our community. I was not.

I continued to receive hate just for being Jewish. After a column I wrote in support of child-free women, I was accused online of 'wanting to stop other women from having children so you can populate the world with your genocidal Jewish babies'.

I quit social media entirely.

I'm a fairly resilient person, but my experience of antisemitism, and of being silenced when I wanted to speak against it, changed me. My passion for writing was crushed. My sense of security was shattered. I learned that antisemitism is just bubbling away under the surface. Friends can turn against me. The community I live in can turn toxic. People will hate me just because I'm Jewish. I have learned, too, that the trauma of persecution is in our DNA, even in those of us who have lived a relatively sheltered life. We cannot escape our trauma, because it continues to play out. We exist in a state of threat, as we have existed for thousands of years. Our history will be denied. Our pain will be mocked. Our words will be twisted and weaponised against us.

More than a year after October 7, my mental health has improved, but my life will never be the same. I cannot unlearn this new knowledge. I will never forget what has happened, and what is still happening. I am still struggling enormously to write anything, including this essay. And as I do, I brace myself for the worst, for these words may be weaponised too.

WHO WILL HIDE MY DAUGHTER?

GALIT KLAS

I am far away from home in the weeks after October 7, staying with my French partner's family in the south of France. It's a big event, having us stay; cousins and friends come through most evenings for long meals and nostalgic conversations. Everyone tries to make me feel comfortable – I'm a new addition to the family; the exotic Australian, and Jewish too. They buy me turkey bacon for crepe night.

My hosts don't mention the news at all. Not because they are tiptoeing around me, but because in their hectic lives the Middle East doesn't count for much. In some ways it's a relief, but I crave connection with someone I can talk to freely and unburden my grief. Someone who gets it: the fear, the paralysis, the disbelief.

I arrange to meet a Chabad rebbetzin in the area. It's a blind date of sorts. I know her sister from Melbourne and when I see her it feels instantly like we are family. We walk around Montpellier and speak Yiddish. We could just as well, and more easily, speak English. But today talking in Yiddish feels fitting. It's a language almost destroyed by the Nazis and I belong to a small group of people worldwide who still use it. Today, Yiddish is a symbol of Jewish survival at a time when Jewish people are again under attack. I relish the opportunity to converse in this tongue, which I studied at university and made the focus of my theatre work for a decade. The familiar cadence of the rebbetzin's voice is healing, her expressive hand gestures comfort my broken heart. So does the Jewishness she infuses into everything – the gratitude she finds in dark moments, the warm way she speaks of her family and the trust she has in God. I need this respite from my generally secular life. At the end of our rendezvous, with a shake in her voice, the rebbetzin encourages me to recite psalms for the release of the hostages. 'That's one thing we can do,' she says.

The reality of the situation in Israel develops slowly, like a polaroid. Music festival. Kibbutzim. Murder. Mutilation. Rape. Hostages – their faces reduced to a small square in a montage of slain and kidnapped innocents. Kfir Bibas, the chubby ten-month-old baby, is only a little older than my daughter. Writing his name feels blasphemous. It has come to symbolise much more than a baby's name should. I should not know of him. In the small bedroom where we are staying, furnished with dream catchers and crystals, my daughter suckles innocently on my breast. I hold her close and weep.

For my theatre work I have researched the often-grim Jewish history extensively and have come to understand that a holocaust is possible anywhere. No community is immune from such a descent into hell. Now, I worry it could be around the corner. And if there is a holocaust in Australia, who can I call on when my workplace stops hiring Jews? When my bank account is frozen. When a soldier appears at the end of my street. When they herd us into ghettos. Post-October 7, these scenarios no longer appear farfetched. More importantly, I need to find a solution for my daughter; I need to be able to keep her safe.

'What would we do if war broke out in Australia?' I ask my partner. 'Where would we go?' He supposes that he would join the resistance. We agree that our daughter and I would hide or flee to a safe country. New Zealand perhaps. For him this discussion is fanciful, for me it's a crisis.

I think of *The Jewish Wife,* Brecht's one-act play set during World War II. The wife calls her German husband's friends, making arrangements for her husband to be looked after while she disappears, so as not to become a liability. Could I be as selfless as that? And would my partner watch me walk away, as the German husband did? I try to believe that my partner would never let me go.

What of my closest friends? Exceptionally intelligent and highly educated women, Labor/Greens supporters, socially conscious. We have a lot in common; the main differences are my Jewish heritage and that I pursued the arts, whereas they built careers in policy and law. I recall the political discussions about the Israeli-Palestinian conflict we had when we were teenagers. I used to think of those conversations as heated exchanges of youthful ideas, as arguments that broadened our perspectives and deepened our understanding of one another. But now I also remember the way they dismissed me as ignorant when our views didn't align, and how staunchly they condemned Israel. I see those conversations through a different lens now – one that highlights a dangerous contempt for Israel particularly among the highly educated. These left-leaning and critically thinking women whom I love… We've been friends for decades, we've celebrated birthdays, weddings and the births of our children. But would they stand by my side if a war broke out? A sad realisation washes through me: no, I can't assume they would come to my aid. I had two friends contact me after October 7; their two messages, like electronic hugs, amplified the silence of the rest.

The question races through my head and won't leave: who will hide my daughter?

During the Holocaust many parents found safety for their children by hiding them with non-Jewish families. Some of the children assumed new names and identities and never saw their families again. Anything for survival. My own Yiddish teacher was a child survivor, kept safely hidden with a non-Jewish family. It feels imperative now that I decide who I can entrust my daughter to, if it becomes unsafe for her to stay with me.

The French village is quiet, but the house is chaotic as the evening dinner preparations unfold. In the bedroom, among the dreamcatchers, I'm settling my daughter for bed. The lullaby I sing to her peters out as my deranged mind conjures up scenes where I plead with my friends, even offering them money for her board and food. I look at my child's features, trying to decide whether she could pass as one of theirs. And if she was raised by someone else, would she ever remember me? In my state, I'm closer than I would like to admit to the cosplaying university students camped in Gaza-like tent cities in the safety of their campuses. I finally decide which friend I would turn to. But what if she refuses? I choose a second-best option – another friend who potentially could raise my daughter as their own. Gradually, my desperation is replaced by a steadfast sense of accomplishment. I have a plan in place.

For the next four weeks of our French sojourn, I read the news often, glued to my phone, as if being perpetually informed will ward off more bad news. We are on a holiday, but the Israel-Hamas war is all I talk about to my partner.

As our date of return draws nearer, I start to also worry about what will happen in Australia. My friends have arranged a dinner and will surely want to talk about 'the war'. Knowing I have close family all over Israel, at the very least they will ask me what I think of the situation. My bones stiffen as I think about this impending conversation which, in my imagination, starts innocuously, then builds into a heated and one-sided attack of my spiritual home, and of me. I am a starry-eyed peacenik, and my heart breaks for the suffering of Palestinians. How could it not? But I also feel the precarious position Israel finds itself in and worry that my friends will believe some of the more extreme accusations, such as that Israel specifically targets hospitals or journalists. I start screenshotting anything that will help me to discuss the war. I save articles with insights I trust, the kind you don't see in the Australian mainstream press.

When I return to Melbourne, I join my closest group of friends for dinner at a Vietnamese place in Richmond. I enter the restaurant with an overly joyous smile to mask my anxiety over what, I fear, might be our last dinner. I sit down, my pram next to me, screenshots at the ready on my phone. My friends wrap me in big hugs and squeal when I show them my new engagement ring. Nobody mentions a thing about the war…

THE CRACK AND THE LIGHT

MELINDA JONES

It's strange how the mind works. For me, October 7 2023 actually began back in October 2016, when I took part in the *March of Hope*. All I have felt and all I have thought about since October 7, with my emotions spiralling out of control, stems back to the day of that march.

The event was organised by Women Wage Peace, a grassroots organisation at the forefront of the Israeli peace movement. It was a march for women who demanded to be included in the peace process, who believed that Jews and Arabs must be able to work together to achieve reconciliation. 30,000 Israeli women – Jews, Christians and Muslims – and 3,000 Palestinian women from Israel, Gaza and the West Bank gathered together. I, a fifth-generation Australian Jew, happened to be in Israel because I was on the International LIMMUD (informal Jewish education) circuit. A maverick scholar, I had just presented my research on the Jewish thought of Leonard Cohen. It was fate that I was in Israel at the time of a march that directly appealed to my politics.

I've always thought of myself as a feminist modern orthodox Jewish woman and a socialist Zionist. I consider culture and religion a heritage to be embraced, but only in the wider context of human rights. I know deep down that Israel is my homeland and I also know that sharing the land is vital – and this has affected everything I've done in my life. From my career as a human rights lawyer, before there was a name for such a thing, to my choice of children's school. So, I decided to go on the march.

The day was long and exhilarating. We travelled from the Jordan River to Jerusalem – taking buses to minimise the distance. All those hours we spent marching, we talked to the women around us, building relationships across cultures and ages. We communicated as best we could, sometimes with hand gestures and sometimes laughing. There were arguments, and no one denied that we were only at the beginning of a process. And yet, on that road, I became certain that peace was real and possible. I felt at one with these women, so much like me for all our differences. I even met Vivian Silver, one of the two charismatic founders of Women Wage Peace. Who would have thought then that in seven years it would take eight days to find enough of her DNA to declare her murdered on October 7.

It was quite incredible that we ended the evening singing Leonard Cohen's Hallelujah in English, Arabic and Hebrew. The song captures the spirit of longing for ultimate resolution, but it is full of ambivalence and hesitation grown from dealing with real people who are never perfect. It inspires us to have faith, whether it is in 'the holy' or maybe in 'the broken, hallelujah'. Sung by thousands of women sharing the same dream that night, the song was my siren calling. Soon I became active in the Israeli women's peace movement and in the Jerusalem-based feminist NGO, the Kiverstein Institute.

That rally was in 2016. The peace. The dream. The 'other' was no longer other – the threat dissipated through respectful conversation.

And through trust. That there was no threat from one people to another. Of course, the process of peace building would be bumpy. But there was a belief within me that honest negotiation was possible. That the Jewish people had partners who also longed for peace. That there were many, many Arab women who wished for the same things as their Jewish allies: a good life with their families, a secure life with neighbours they could share recipes with.

***

In the last eight years, I've worked with others to spread knowledge and build relations within the peace movement internationally, with the Australian feminist movement, and between Jews and Arabs in Israel. I've been involved in projects like Praying Together in Jerusalem, which brings Jews, Christians and Muslims together monthly; and in the production of an interfaith/intercultural film on Security Council Resolution 1325 which demands women's involvement in the peace process.

It took several years, while the organisation grew, for another massive march to be organised by Women Wage Peace and Women of the Sun (Women Wage Peace's counterpart operating from Palestinian territories). I went to Jerusalem and the Dead Sea on October 4, 2023, representing Australia. Hundreds of the 45,000 women who are members of the organisations participated. The core document, The Mothers' Call, was adopted by the movement leadership and the international representation. It said: 'We, Palestinian and Israeli mothers, are determined to stop the vicious cycle of bloodshed and to change the reality of the difficult conflict between both nations, for the benefit of our children.' I was a true believer. Peace was in the air. It was palpable.

Three days later.

Simchat Torah.

October 7 – a crack in my coat of hope.

There were air raid sirens in Jerusalem that day. It couldn't be real, but that night on national TV I saw revellers running for their lives at the Nova music festival. Shot and piled body on body in air raid shelters. I saw kibbutzim that had been invaded. I saw burnt bodies and children shot in front of their parents. The evidence of sexual violence, with bloodied girls and mutilated women. And the two little red-headed boys taken hostage.

Everybody I knew, knew someone who was directly affected. My daughter-in-law's uncle was missing for three days. My sister's colleague and my niece's babysitter were murdered on their kibbutz. My daughter's friend was at the Nova festival and had escaped with her life. My parents-in-law's house took a direct hit from a rocket. My nephew's best friend remains among the kidnapped, dead or alive. And a close Australian friend's cousin was taken hostage in her pyjamas, dragged away in bloody pants. The country was somehow holding itself together and at the same time, its people were unravelling. I was unravelling.

When I need comforting or am seeking wisdom, I often turn to Cohen's songs and poems, where the Jewish concept of *Tikkun Olam*, the drive to repair the world and leave it a better place, is central, as it is in my life. According to the Kabbalah, this task involves finding wayward shafts of light that have escaped from holy vessels, and returning them to their source. The darkness surrounds the light. It overwhelms the light. But sometimes there are cracks in the darkness. The beauty of the crack is that it creates a place where the light gets in. The existence of this light is hope for peace, as Cohen tells it. The darkness does not have to win. But I didn't see any light on or after October 7. Only darkness everywhere. The darkness in which I ruminated: can those Arab women I worked with just a few days earlier be trusted? Am I a fool to believe they are partners in peace?

***

A year later, and many of the people who had been my colleagues, fellow travellers and allies in the world of human rights and social justice, are no longer such. It was particularly painful to see how the feminist movement, including many of my friends, responded to October 7. They took two inconsistent positions, one involving justification of what happened and the other denial.

The first is so weird that I still can't get my head around it. Hamas posted videos of their atrocious violence from GoPro cameras during the pogrom. One terrorist rang his mother, jubilant, saying he had just killed his tenth Jew – 'praised be Allah'. Men were the violators; women were the victims of horrific sexual violence. It was not so long ago that rape in war was recognised as a war crime, as the world is reminded annually on the International Day for the Elimination of Sexual Violence in Conflict. But, according to some of my feminist ex-friends, 'rape is resistance'. Somehow the women who were abused, deserved it.

The other feminist response was even more frightening. For years now feminists have argued that we must believe women about sexual assault, because it is the sort of stuff that people don't just make up. That's what the #metoo movement was about. So how come so many seemingly intelligent and compassionate people – public officials, activists, my once friends – deny the claim, despite all the evidence, that there was sexual violence perpetrated by Hamas? It seems that it is now #metoo unless you're a Jew.

***

Cracks or not, I continue to build a presence for Women Wage Peace in Australia. Now everything is on a different scale. I'm frantic. There is so much political work to be done. I attend rallies, vigils, protests, demonstrations. Some are for Israel with prayers for survival. Others focus on the hostages, invoking their names or sharing the pain of family members.

I address the final annual conference of the Equality Rights Alliance, an Australian women's peak body I've been part of for years. I give an impassioned speech on the international feminist response to October 7, the situation in Gaza and the antisemitism that is making Jewish people so vulnerable even in the paradise that is, or rather was, Australia. This is my opportunity to publicly express my sorrow. Sorrow about the attacks on women who happen to be Jews, antisemitism mouthed by 'antiracist activists', the promotion of war and hatred by those claiming to be peace activists. Afterwards, several people come and give me hugs. But many more, most, stare at me with animosity. These used to be *my people*.

I don't know where to put myself. Do I have to shed everything I've believed about myself to fit anywhere? Am I still a left-wing warrior? Is it possible for anyone to be left wing and pro-Israel? But if not, how is it that I see no inconsistency between the belief in the rights of Jews and the belief in the rights of Arabs to be treated with dignity and respect? How is it possible to be committed to social justice and to care for all of humanity, bar one group?

Socialist Zionism has never been about building a Jewish state at all costs. My values, I have to remind myself these days, are sound.

I've lost my bearings and lost faith in humanity, because cracks are everywhere now. The world is no longer based on an agreed definition of words. Facts have lost their currency. What counts is the identity of the speaker. But not Jews, as the English-Jewish writer David Baddiel persuasively argues, because 'Jews don't count'.

American-Jewish author Dara Horn thinks that the only Jews that non-Jews like are dead Jews. Well, I'm staying alive till my time. And I'll continue working for sense to prevail. I notice it's not just me who is possessed by this feeling of urgency to do something. So many other Jewish people seem to be taken by activism. The effect of October 7 seems to have been felt by every Jew. So perhaps Leonard Cohen is right and there really has been some light coming through all those cracks. While my fear tells me that I should not trust – it is too risky – deep down I know that there can be no solutions unless we find a way to trust. We must have partners in peace to rebuild the land we share, as the socialist Zionist in me imagines it.

A RANT AND A RECIPE

LISA GOLDBERG

I am a home cook. Cooking and eating, and obsessively talking about cooking and eating, have always been an enormous part of my life thanks to three things: my DNA, the man I married who loves food more than life itself, and the *Monday Morning Cooking Club* cookbook project, a series of books I produced as part of a wonderful sisterhood of six co-authors. Since 2006, we have collected and published recipes and stories from our Jewish community to preserve its culinary traditions for future generations.

Social media gave me the perfect vehicle to share my food obsession as well as promote our project. I'd snap and post images of the exceptional schnitzel sandwich at S'wich in Bondi or a perfect martini on a Sunday afternoon at Totti's; I'd make videos of buttery, crisp-shelled, just-doughy croissants in Paris; and flaky molten-custard Portuguese tarts in Lisbon. Instagram was my way to showcase the Monday Morning Cooking Club and to inspire people to cook with confidence and joy. My cafe visits, travel videos and mouthwatering food content helped create a food community, building a nice following of more than 32,000 people.

Then came October 7. Disbelief, death and destruction. The hostages. Celebrations in Western Sydney. Violent words and flames on the Opera House steps. Inexplicable hate directed at my people. The ground beneath me began to give way, as did my social media world.

Several days after October 7, I attended the very first Sydney prayer vigil organised by the Jewish community, where I stood side by side with 10,000 others to commemorate victims of the Hamas massacre. I shared a short video of the event on Instagram, tagging #istandwithisrael. Cue hate-filled comments and 2000 unfollows. It was a sad moment. Sounds a little unhinged now, but my initial reaction was to make *cholent*, the ultimate Jewish centuries-old comfort food: slow cooked beef, beans, barley and potato. Together, on Instagram Live, a random group of mostly Jewish home cooks, united in grief, cooked the dish as a soul-soothing reminder of the old world, of our ancestral communities standing together and standing strong despite hardship. The response was much love and support, and, at the same time, more unfollows.

I became all-consumed with social media's role in spreading antisemitism, anti-Zionism and sheer hate, against the terrifying backdrop of the hostages still in Gaza and the devastating loss of so many innocent lives on all sides of the conflict. In the face of it all, my online habits started to shift. I began obsessively searching for everything related to Israel and the Jewish diaspora. I stopped posting what I was eating. I started posting about Israel. I was learning so much every day – about Israel's history, the Palestinian story, jihadism and the Iranian axis of evil – and I wanted to share what I discovered. Surprisingly, I became braver as the weeks went by and, unsurprisingly, received more hate. 'Go to hell, Grandma,' did make me laugh. Of course, that was not the worst of it.

When I resumed posting about food, I did it differently. I decided to use food as a way to share advocacy messages, promising a 'rant and a recipe'. Come for the food, stay for the activist inspiration.

I made my Shabbat 'essential', egg and onion, to tell the story of tradition, of a recipe passed down from my grandmother, which reflects the longevity and strength of our people. I baked our *Monday Morning Cooking Club* classic chocolate chiffon cake, showing viewers step-by-step how to cut the cake out of the tin, while imploring them to address the elephant in the room: Hamas is an internationally recognised terror group, not 'freedom fighters' as portrayed by some social media influencers. For Chanukah, I fried latkes in oil – a custom celebrating a Jewish victory that reclaimed Jerusalem back from the Greek Seleucid empire more than 2000 years ago. And in another video, I kneaded challah, feeling Jewish pride with each fist of dough, urging everyone to speak out against Jew-hatred.

The food world post-October 7 is a different universe for me now. In an industry underpinned by respect for other cultures and places, I assumed that everyone I dealt with was on the same page as me in respect of those matters. But now I am heartbroken that so many chefs and cooks, who I used to revere, are unable to have a civil conversation with me about the war, are unable to see past their inexplicable, irrational hate of Zionists. Do they even know what this contested word means? The anti-Israel movement's 'Zionist' is a dehumanised caricature, someone who supports a genocide that Israel is supposedly perpetrating. In reality, a Zionist is simply someone who believes that Israel has a right to exist as a homeland for the Jewish people. So you can be a Zionist and also care about Palestinian rights, and being a Zionist doesn't necessitate supporting every decision of the Israeli government.

Initially, I tried to engage in civil debates with my peers. One chef, who I had a decades-long relationship with, made a post comparing the Holocaust with the situation in Gaza, and equating the Nazis with Israel. It was a kick in my guts. I emailed, explaining in the nicest possible way why her post was antisemitic and why she may want to rethink it. Her reply was insulting and dismissive of my lived experience as a Jew. She was 'disgusted by the genocide of Palestinians', continuing, predictably: 'I am certainly not anti-semetic [sic], but am anti-Zionist – so we will have to agree to disagree here.'

Another chef responded to my (polite) challenge to his uninformed anti-Israel posts: 'I'm really not interested in Zionist propaganda…There's no need for you to reply.'

The online food world is rife with anti-Zionist slogans and anti-'Israhell' propaganda, and it is hard to bear. Even harder to bear is real life, where, for example, the owner of a well-known group of restaurants recently paraded in the street with a homemade placard displaying an Israeli flag, with the Star of David replaced with a swastika. (He was charged under new legislation – no swastikas are allowed in NSW.)

In another challenging real-life example, early in 2023 I created a ten-part YouTube food show, *Walking up an Appetite*, where I walked, ate and cooked (my three favourite pastimes) my way across Sydney. Each episode was dedicated to a particular dish; I visited three eateries that offered the dish and interviewed the chef. The falafel episode was the most difficult to set up.

For the initial research to find my favourite falafel, I went to falafel shops in Lakemba, Bass Hill, Punchbowl, North Bexley, Newtown and Marrickville. I was always welcomed, yet when my production team sought permission to include those places in the show, we found it was harder to get a yes than for the other episodes. At the time, I didn't even think about why. Eventually, we managed to confirm three eateries and the filming schedule was fixed. Two days before filming, the first place cancelled. The second cancelled the following day and, on the day of filming, our contact at the third venue didn't show up.

I tried not to take the difficulties personally. I didn't think about it again and the episode was released in mid-2023 (it ended up being the only episode with no chef interviews and with two rather than three filmed eatery visits). Fast forward to post-October 7, when the world changed. One chef, the creator of a particularly good and unique falafel pita, the one who cancelled two days before filming, posted online, ostensibly addressing a pro-Israel person: '...hope you, your entire "state" and every single [person] within gets obliterated. [Everyone] collectively hates Israel, now and forever.' Another – whose falafel I rated highly and whose place did feature in the episode – posted that 'narcissistic Zionist pigs' should 'f**k off' and were not welcome at their place.

These comments, although not directed at me personally, were a startling affront. Did I have all those issues with the falafel episode because I was Jewish? It makes you think. Ironically, I had always thought that the evolution of the falafel, starting in Alexandria and moving across the Middle East, was evidence that food could be a way to bring people together across cultures.

Some days I feel overwhelmed by the hate circulating in my industry. I've grown hesitant in my personal interactions. Now, when I am contacted for a recipe or a post, I first check the person's social media for hints of Jew-hatred before I proceed. It's hard to believe we are living in a world where that seems necessary.

I also ask myself every so often: am I doing something worthwhile online? I know I am not changing those minds that can't be changed, but I hope I am at least speaking out for those who feel they have no voice and sometimes inspiring just a few to stand up and be strong.

Even during these dark days, there is a silver lining. I have never felt more connected to my people. I have been collecting recipes and stories for almost twenty years and have never felt prouder to do so. To share our recipes as they are passed from generation to generation, through exile and immigration, through grief and joy. To tell the stories of our people as they have been told for millennia.

Our community in Australia is strong and resilient, and continuity is certain. But, silver lining aside, I look forward to the day when my most controversial post can be about whether or not it is acceptable to eat butter on a croissant.

PACING THE STAGE

DEBORAH CONWAY

On October 3 2023, I released a memoir, *Book of Life*. Four days later the world changed.

On October 7 we were in the middle of a matinee performance of *Songs from the Book of Life*, an accompanying show for my memoir, at Arts Centre Melbourne. We were playing our fourth show, had shaken off the nerves, and were enjoying ourselves along with our audience who were laughing in all the right places. Apart from a brief exit to add some bells and whistles to my costume, I spent most of the performance on stage; there was no interval. Willy Zygier, my artistic collaborator and husband, got to exit the stage at various moments while I delivered monologues. On one of his backstage jaunts, he saw a message from our youngest daughter who was living in Tel Aviv. It was obtuse: 'Don't worry, I'm sheltering in the stairwell of my apartment.' Willy wrote back trying to understand what was going on, then checked X. Information was scant, as it would be for a number of hours.

We remained at the theatre, believing that it was just another of the Hamas rocket barrages that invade Israeli airspace from Gaza at frequent intervals but do little damage because of Israeli anti-missile defences. I remember being relatively confident that the skirmish would be over within a matter of days.

Our show is a three-dimensional theatrical and musical distillation of my life with sets, props, interactive footage and choreography composed of eight scenes. Scene four is a discussion of my Jewishness; a discussion that, by its very nature, has to include a brief analysis of antisemitism. It was something Willy and I had been witnessing for several decades – hate, moving inexorably with the gathering pace of a stampeding herd. This excerpt from our show was very direct. After the matinee performance of October 7, it became an existential howl.

> *The history of the Jew lurches through chapter and verse of persecution for multitudes of contradictory reasons. We are the wandering Jew, the rootless cosmopolitan, we are the outsider; we are the controllers of finance and industry, of Hollywood and the media, we are the insider; we are insular, infiltrators, untrustworthy, ready to break our vows, we're arrogant, G-d's chosen, pushy, weak, loud, stealthy, communist, capitalist, once too oriental, now too white. Antisemitism motivates its adherents to attribute to the Jew whatever their society deems its most detestable qualities. And throughout history Jews pay with blood. Maybe all a Jew can do is pace the stage and pray.*

There I was, a Jew, pacing the stage while our 23-year-old daughter was experiencing a rocket barrage. My darling youngest daughter is a party animal and if she had not recently split with her Israeli boyfriend, they might have both been at the Nova festival.

The revelations about the October 7 massacre that started to emerge were unbearable, but the response from around the world was a deep dive into Dante's Inferno. The denials of Hamas' atrocities; the victim blaming; the reframing of savage barbarity into resistance; the cries of ~~gas the Jews~~, sorry, fuck the Jews, on the steps of the Sydney Opera House while angry men burn Israeli flags and dance in celebration for the latest chapter of 'Globalise the Intifada'. All this before Israel had lifted so much as a finger in response, before the 1200 bodies were cold or identified, before anyone had figured out who was kidnapped and who was a dismembered pile of human remains.

Overnight, any Jew who supported Israel's right to exist – i.e. a Zionist – became a figure of hate. It didn't take long for left-wing radicals to join forces with Islamists and adopt old blood libels for a new millennium. Zionists became interchangeable with Nazis, baby killers, promoters of genocide; the pre-packaged slurs came right out of the Elders of Zion playbook or the medieval Christian playbook. Ancient yet somehow completely on trend.

The betrayal was so thorough. The believe-all-women feminists suddenly needed proof from rape victims they'd been raped; apparently, nails shot into genitals just wasn't cutting it. The footage, filmed by the perpetrators, was not enough. Conspiracy theories were gleefully circulated that the IDF had, in fact, murdered most of the victims. So, there you have it, not 'gas the Jews' but 'gaslight the Jews'.

My head was spinning. Despite the tsunami of antisemitism, no one was coming to their senses. Where were the adults in the room? They were too busy making calculations on marginal seats and where votes might be won or lost. Moral compass be damned.

All the Jews I knew were despairing, confused. So were we. In November, Willy and I played at Mushroom Record's widely watched 50th birthday celebration wearing white suits and blue shirts; he wore a yarmulke, I wore my oversized Magen David. We did it to show solidarity, to announce we wouldn't be intimidated. It was good to be able to do something after weeks of feeling utterly impotent. An outpouring of support came, from Jews in particular who saw it as a fist in the air. But we also attracted threatening commentary along the lines of, 'Hey genocide supporters, nice white suits you got there, pity if they got covered in blood.' Those comments were the opening shots, delineating the propaganda war we'd stepped into.

In December I was invited to talk to Patricia Karvelas on Radio National about the equivalence, if there was any, between the controversy of the Sydney Theatre Company actors donning keffiyehs for their encore bows, and Willy and I dressing as we had for the Mushroom event. Within a few minutes, the conversation turned to Gaza with Ms Karvelas questioning me about the high death toll of young people. The next few moments became ground zero for my fall from grace.

The haters decoupled my very few words (seven to be exact) from the context of their intent, waving them as a flag to proclaim my craven disregard for human suffering. The meaning of my words in context is: Hamas' use of underage boys as fighters and then as part of the childhood casualty count is a horrendous, cynical exploitation of young lives. The mountain of evidence[1] for this 'strategy' remains unexamined by those who see Hamas as 'freedom fighters'.

So, there I was: a new book – my first book – and a full dance card of author talks, in-conversations and writers' festivals. Officially, I was about to embark on a wonderful adventure, unofficially I had become a slavering, blood-thirsty, child-murdering genocide supporter.

At first the cancellations dribbled in, then they picked up pace.

Charity events, radio shows, podcasts, all cancelled.

I should point out that my book is a memoir of an Australian musician, not a treatise on the Middle East.

Little Bird Bookshop in Brisbane hastily organised an in-conversation to promote my book, and a gathering of furious activists turned up on a quiet suburban street to scream in our faces and pound on the glass. A dozen police attended but did nothing to shut down the protest.

Many writers' festivals, patronised by people who proclaim themselves to be warriors for the exchange of free ideas, were perfectly happy to shut down views or speakers that a few disrupters could find offensive. There were writers' festivals that did stand by me, though some of them were forced to employ a phalanx of security. Others walked back their invitations. I don't know if I blame them or not, but the reasons given for cancellation sounded disingenuous to me. Organisers of one NSW-based literary event I had been booked to open, for example, claimed their event had to be cancelled for health reasons, though strangely it went ahead, just without me. The Byron Writers Festival booked me, then retracted their invitation with an alternative offer to schedule an out-of-festival event. A few months later they cancelled that too. No adequate reason was offered.

Our theatre shows were also targeted. Like with writers' festivals, some promoters cancelled, while others hired security for our protection. The Hobart Playhouse performance was a new low. Outside, protesters handed out pamphlets detailing my villainy. Inside, activists disrupted our show repeatedly, having to be forcibly removed from the theatre until eventually a patron decided to take matters into her own hands, break her wine glass on the edge of the stage and use it to threaten a protester who was yelling that I was a disgusting monster. The ensuing mayhem was a glimpse into societal breakdown.

Then there was the silence, the events that simply didn't materialise though I was sure they would.

A few months back, I heard *Tablet* and *New York Times* columnist (and Jew) Brett Stephens address a Jewish audience. Someone asked how he was managing the high levels of hostility. 'I get a bit more Jewy every day,' he said. I completely got it. So had I. So had most of the Jews I know. We had all gotten a bit more Jewy. Wearing visible Magen Davids, lighting Shabbat candles, seeking out each other's company, reading Jewish authors and Israeli newspapers, attending Jewish cultural events.

Since October 7, the world where no one cared if I was a Jew or not has fundamentally shifted. It's hard to convey how profound this change has been. Historical posters of Willy's and my shows have been graffitied and then pulled off the walls in a Melbourne venue we have played many times over the years. The last couple of times we played in Sydney, I was confronted with 'D. CONWAY IS A ZIONIST STOOGE' graffiti scrawled over the walls outside the venue. Every time we post on social media, we are hyper-aware of the trolls writing vile, sometimes threatening commentary. Horrifically, this is the new normal.

These days I feel wary whenever I meet someone new, wondering whether my reputation precedes me. I've grown cautious as to how I express myself. The trip wires are everywhere.

I don't know what will happen next. Something has broken and I don't see a way towards repairing the distrust that has engulfed our lives. Willy and I channel our creative energies into songs that address the current state of the world, we're having a purple patch. We are still as poetically blatant about our positions as we have been since we released our album *Stories of Ghosts* in 2013. I introduce those songs by saying: '*Stories of Ghosts* is a series of dialogues around themes from the Old Testament from an atheist Jewish perspective. It's our Jewish record, everyone should have one.' When I make this introduction these days, I'm not as confident that someone won't throw something at me.

On the flip side, I am buoyed by the enormous support we have received from the many people whose moral compass is, I believe, perfectly intact. I continue to pace the stage. If I'm ducking verbal projectiles as I do, so be it.

---

1   See eg.
    Ahmed Fouad Alkhatib, 'The Origin of Hamas' Human Shields Strategy in Gaza', *Newsweek*, 26 February 2024.
    Brad Sherman, 'You're Being Misled About the Gaza Death Toll', *Newsweek*, 10 January 2024.
    Seth J. Frantzman, 'Hamas Continues Recruiting Child Soldiers: Where is the Condemnation?', *Jerusalem Post*, 27 June 2021.

POLICE REPORT

NINA SANADZE

From: ▮▮▮▮ Criminal Investigation Unit
Senior Constable ▮▮▮▮ 1599
Station: ▮▮▮▮ Police Station
Report Number: ▮▮▮▮
Date: 19 February 2024

Victim Information:
The victim, NS, is a 48-year-old sculptor of Jewish ethnicity, born in Soviet Georgia and currently residing in Melbourne. She has been a resident artist at a government-funded gallery studio program for approximately eighteen months, with half a year remaining to the end of her tenure. Prior to the incident, NS held a positive reputation both professionally and personally.

Incident Description:
On 8 October 2023, following the October 7 massacre carried out by Hamas, the victim shared blurred images on Instagram depicting the mutilated body of Shani Louk, and the faces of other Israeli women who were taken hostage. In addition, the victim posted a quote attributed to Golda Meir: 'If Arabs put down their guns, there would be no more fighting. If the Israelis put down theirs, there would be no more Israel.'

> NS: Broken body, hers and mine. Red eyes swollen, hers and mine.

Following these posts, the victim experienced online harassment, verbal abuse and aggression from neighbouring studio artists. Studio management received denunciation letters from the victim's colleagues and former friends, accusing her of betraying the progressive arts community. Some individuals circulated social media posts about the victim, labelling her a 'traitorous snake' and a 'dirty Zionist'. Others demanded her removal from the studio residency program, going so far as to call her a 'genocidal Nazi Zionist'.

> NS: Loud, menacing protests erupt; burning flags light the streets as chants of 'F*** the Jews' echo. No time to mourn. Cups overflow with tears, fear – thick and suffocating – takes its hold. Hide.

In November 2023, one of the new resident artists vacated their studio in protest against the residency for hosting a Zionist. This led to further outrage, with other artists calling the victim a 'dangerous racist', 'bully' and 'harasser' who should have left instead.

> NS: *The friendliest person in the office, the one with the dog, is the first and only one to check on me since the October 7 tragedy. She offers a hug as I cry. 'You're not a bad person,' she says.*

Management met with the victim to state that they did not condone the behaviour of the involved artists or the harassment she had faced. However, they advised her to 'read the room' and avoid interacting with others in the studio.

> NS: *I arrive early and leave late. I used to leave the door ajar, but now I lock it, particularly fearful of some of the neighbouring artists. The director recently shut it from the outside so as not to disturb others with my presence. I avoid the toilet. I whisper when I make phone calls. Later, I read in an article that antisemitism historically follows a predictable pattern: it begins with harassment, followed by isolation and ultimately culminates in violence.*

The studio board faced growing pressure to issue a public statement on the 'genocide in Gaza'. Artists were invited to share their perspectives. While everyone supported the motion, the victim submitted an open letter titled Death of Art, advocating for the gallery's neutrality.

> NS: *I join a new, supportive community of Jewish creatives – a small island, a WhatsApp group. Some names familiar, most not. Hundreds of stories fill my days – some of them are reaffirming, others reinforce my worst fears about global attitudes towards Jews in the arts.*

In December 2023, a member of the studio management shared a story on social media inviting others to join a 'friendly' Sunday rally. The victim commented, expressing interest in attending the rally if it was about peace, but also mentioning feeling unsafe due to some slogans displayed at previous rallies. The individual blocked the victim and subsequently filed a complaint of harassment.

> NS: *Desperate, I post an image of a blank white paper, a white flag – space for new slogans, for peace. Out with extreme governments on both sides, peace and safety for all civilians. Comments flood in. Most say: Israel should not exist.*

On 18 January 2024, a member of an Australia-wide Jewish creatives and academics WhatsApp group, a New York Times journalist, downloaded private conversations from the chat. The 900 pages were shared with anti-Zionist activists, leading to a mass doxing and harassment campaign, 'Zio600', starting on 30 January 2024. Also, a list containing work details, photos and contact information was distributed to over half a million people to target individuals. The victim was listed among the 'top 30', singled out as a primary target for harassment and career destruction.

> NS: *The morning after my 48th birthday, my life dissolved – like a golden carriage turning into a pumpkin. My father, an orchestra conductor, had died at 48 from a broken heart, after a year of bullying and betrayal at his workplace that ensued when a colleague schemed to take his job. I had always feared this age, as if it held some dark magic, and it did.*

On 31 January 2024, the victim was interrogated by management in a laneway, during which they reviewed the pages of transcripts from the leaked chat. The management inquired about other 'Zionist groups' the victim may belong to. The victim was instructed not to attend the studio without prior notification to all management.

On 1 February 2024, an emergency meeting of resident artists (excluding the victim), management and the board was called. A message was later sent, informing the victim that her presence in the studio would be considered 'inappropriate'. She was advised not to return. The studio became a site of protest, with stickers covering the façade and large graffiti, 'Zio Dogs', defacing the entrance.

> *NS: Two weeks in bed; it's hard to walk. My gallerist tells me she cannot defend me, it's too unsafe. Her eyes are filled with tears as she delivers the henchman's final decree: we must part.*

On 18 February 2024, the victim was summoned to a meeting with the studio management in the gallery, where the setting was altered to resemble a Soviet-era-style tribunal. The exhibition's pink wall paintings and crystal stone sculptures were obscured by a large table at the front, draped in black cloth, with the gallery studio residency directors seated behind it, papers in hand, poised to deliver their judgement. The session began with management instructing the victim not to reference her ethnicity or personal history during the proceedings. She was accused of being a 'bully, racist and harasser' and was pressured to immediately forfeit her studio residency, for her own good – to avoid fabricated and damaging information about her being spread online again if she resisted. Despite remaining silent throughout the proceedings, the directors repeatedly interjected: 'And don't be a victim.'

Author's note: This essay is based on a police report filed by the author.

IN CASE I EVER GET KIDNAPPED

TAMAR PALUCH

A few years ago, my daughter Amalia, then aged six, found a Magen David necklace at home and told me she'd like to wear it to school. 'I want everyone to know that I'm Jewish,' she said. Bless, I thought. Her school is as Jewish as can be. She had just learnt about the biblical super-heroine, Esther, who had to hide her Jewish identity only to later reveal it to save her people. How lucky we are to live in our times, I mused.

Three years on and our world has been upended. The long shadow of hate, cast by the events of October 7, arrived on our distant shores quickly. Students from Jewish schools now conceal identifying features of their school uniforms and bags on public transport. Some Jews have removed their *mezuzah*, the ritual talisman on their doorpost which marks it a Jewish home.

As much as I try to shield my children, the hate seeps through. We are at a stop sign when Rahni, my five-year-old, cranes her neck to inspect a sticker on it and says, 'Ima, there's an Israeli flag with a red line through it.' She then explains in earnest, 'I think that means they hate Israel.' A few days later, Amalia sees defaced hostage posters at the park and asks, 'But why would someone do that?' I can see her eyes brim with tears, her lip quivers. This is her first encounter with such contempt for human life.

My husband and I don't believe in keeping secrets – for intuitive children, not knowing can be just as scary as knowing. In any case, kids can stumble across distressing information online or be exposed to it through their friends. We think we are clever parents, because we practice the art of framing – carefully choosing when, how and what to explain – but we inevitably leave a hole here and there, and there is nothing as insatiable as a child who knows there is more to know. We try to leapfrog the hate by highlighting the things that show Jewish people as resilient and united. We show the girls videos of displaced Israeli kids receiving gifts from diaspora communities, and take them to a local warehouse where our community volunteers are packing and dispatching huge shipments of presents and needed goods.

We are selective about what we reveal, but as time passes the war is only accelerating, the hostages aren't coming home, and anti-Jewish hate is pulsing across the globe. Our mission feels like a mission impossible. Amalia is haunted by a story she overheard at school about a baby that was found in an oven on October 7. Her cousins call while they are in the bomb shelter, and she asks whether the Iron Dome ever fails. How can we avoid discussing what is happening in her country of birth or what it means to be a Jew, especially an Israeli Jew, in the post-October 7 world? Amalia was born in Jerusalem, just like her father and her grandmother, a fact that she wears as a badge of honour. We don't want to diminish her ancestral pride but worry what might happen if she tells the wrong person where she was born. Usually, we would send her to holiday activities which suit her personality and give her a chance to befriend kids outside of the Jewish community, but we pare back the list of options – no creative arts in Prahran, no coding camp north of the Yarra. We clip her wings for now and send her to a local Jewish camp.

***

I was brought up from a young age with a certain awareness that the world is not to be trusted. My late mother was born and raised in the nascent State of Israel, my father in a German town where concentration camp survivors gathered to look for relatives and friends before resettling in places like Melbourne, the city of my birth. My mother swapped the varied landscapes of Israel for the gumtrees of Australia. She named me after the palm trees of the Sinai Peninsula, which was handed over to Egypt around the time of my birth. She grieved from afar for the desert communities in Sinai, uprooted for the promise of peace with what felt like untrustworthy neighbours. Always dramatic, she said her breast milk ran dry from the tears.

I grew up feeling proud of my hybrid identity and always loved emphasising that my name was the Israeli Tamar, not Tamara, pronounced with an r that rolls off the tongue. As a young child I felt special having two passports, even though my mother – the Entebbe hostage crisis still fresh in her mind – told me to keep one hidden in case our flight was hijacked. I remember how she would sing along wistfully to the music on the Israeli community radio while preparing for Shabbat. Occasionally, I'd hear some shocking news filtering through the airwaves, of wars and suicide bombings in Israel. My mother would frantically call around to check that everyone was safe.

Looking back, my childhood home in peaceful Australia exuded the Israeli spirit of my mother – exuberant, loud, emotional – as well as the quiet, industrious stoicism of the diaspora survivors on my father's side. I was grateful for the way these forces ran through me, and felt they made me strong and ready to take on an unpredictable world. I had hoped that my girls would grow strong too, without having to put their strength to the test.

***

I am on my way out to dinner. Rahni says to me, 'Ima, my babysitters never say *Shema* with me.' Shema is the ultimate Jewish prayer, both an affirmation of faith in one God, and a nighttime prayer that parents recite, beseeching the angels to protect their children. I ask Amalia to say Shema with Rahni that night. 'It doesn't matter if you don't get it 100 percent right,' I say. Last time I checked, she was still fumbling over the words despite having heard them every day since she was born. Amalia's eyes light up and she exclaims proudly, 'It's ok, I have been practising – in case I ever get kidnapped.' My heart drops.

No matter that we stop watching the news in the children's presence, that we speak about the escalating antisemitism in Hebrew and not English. Our attempt to control Amalia's exposure to the chaos in the world is clearly not working. We may have shielded her from the images of October 7, but she is playing reels in her mind that I cannot pause. Several days later, she comes home from school with a 'sensory poem' she penned:

> WORRIED
> Worry is all I can think about.
> It looks like war.
> It sounds like screams.
> It smells like smoke.
> It tastes rotten.

It feels like the hate of another country.

I see it now – kids learn the art of dot-to-dot and fill in the spaces with their imagination. With her grandmother and cousins all living in Israel, the stress of war is ever-present for Amalia, despite the distance. She often asks about the hostages and collects postcards of their faces from our local Jewish grocery store. Some days she is angry that her teachers won't speak about the war; some days she is angry when they do. 'I just want this nightmare to be over!' she rages one day. I say I feel the same way. We talk about despair and hope, and about the power of taking action. I show her the tote bag of KIDNAPPED posters and packing tape that I keep in my car; and the STOP THE HATE stickers and fat textas I use to erase antisemitic graffiti, which sit in my handbag alongside pretzels, fruit straps and hand moisturiser.

A package of yellow ribbons arrives for an event I am organising in support of the hostages. Amalia helps herself to a roll and takes it to school. She comes home excited that she has done something impactful. Apparently, the kids and teachers all wanted a strand of ribbon to pin on their jumper, joining the call to release the hostages. She needs another roll, she says. Together we are finding ways to hold onto hope.

***

If Amalia is our poet-in-residence, then Rahni is our resident problem solver. She has a plan on how to end the war. 'I'll write to Hamas and tell him that he is not nice. If I see him, I'll kick him in the nuts,' she declares. She is not old enough to understand that Hamas is not one person, that it is a pernicious mindset spreading across the globe. That the stickers she spots around town are propaganda, that dehumanisation and demonisation of Jews is a weapon.

Instead, Rahni does what children do – she follows her senses. She starts to see the world through a new colour prism: blue and white are for Israel; yellow is for the hostages; and the combination of green, red and white makes her uneasy. I cautiously point out that many of the world's flags use a mix of these three colours, and that perhaps the only colour she needs to be wary of is the green on the headband worn by Hamas terrorists. She shrugs her shoulders. Discussing degrees of hate is hard to do with a five-year-old, but she listens as I explain the difference between the Palestinian people and Hamas, saying that many Palestinians suffer under Hamas too. From then on she whoops, 'Boo Hamas!' whenever she sees green, and her sister pinches her and tells her to shush in case someone hears. Perhaps I should retract my ill-conceived colour lesson, but instead I laugh at her sweet bravado.

***

I have never felt my identities as a mother and a Jew activated as powerfully and urgently as in these times. The world in which I was once fluent and comfortable feels alien and untrustworthy. I worry endlessly about my husband, with his unmistakable Israeli accent as he keeps travelling abroad for work (though he has stopped flying solo to Europe where the street protests have turned especially vicious). I navigate public spaces with a primitive hyper-vigilance now, especially when my daughters are with me, envious of those who float around without a care, as I once did. Who are these people around us? Friends, foes, fence-sitters? My senses alert, I urgently scan the train station for indicators of possible anti-Jewish hostility, and for the kindest-looking person – someone who would help shield my children if the situation required it.

But who is kind enough these days? When even leading children's and human rights organisations are unwilling to advocate for the world's youngest hostages, Kfir and Ariel Bibas? I fight against my own cynicism to avoid being swallowed by it. How can I teach my children to be defined by who they are and not by the hate around them, when I feel like this? Do I have it in me to teach them not to hate back? I want my girls to navigate the world with the confidence I was gifted – aware of hate, but not afraid the way I am these days. Right now, we Jews are shrinking into ourselves, finding comfort and safety in insularity, but I desperately hope that my girls will re-emerge into a safer, and kinder, world.

NOTHING ANTISEMITIC HERE

NICKY STEIN

Mornings are difficult. I open my eyes. It is October 7 again and again. It has been months since the day that changed everything, but there is a haunting loop in my brain. The blood-stained pants of Naama Levy as she is carted into a jeep, the lifeless and exposed body of Shani Louk on the back of a pickup truck, the forlorn face of Rachel Goldberg as she pleads for her son Hersh's return... I shower and dress. I grab the hostage tags from my bedside table where they lie at night as I sleep, the only time they are not around my neck. I scrawl the number of days the hostages have been in captivity onto some torn masking tape which I fix to my shirt. I pull on the rubber bracelets that I bought early in the conflict, which reassure me: 'Our love will rebuild.'

Perhaps the most difficult part of my morning is watching my oldest son, a first-year student at The University of Sydney, as he gets ready to face his day, bracing himself for the rush of hate. He hugs me as he leaves the house, saying, 'Never again, Mum. Never again'. I had tried to dissuade him from studying at that institution, with its long history of antisemitism. But he was adamant and, like a typical teenager, he was certain his mother was exaggerating. Until his first day at orientation week, when he returned home and instead of launching with his usual enthusiasm into stories about his lecturers or what the campus was like, he handed me the various 'welcome packs' from student bodies, each filled with flyers and stickers spreading anti-Israel hatred. He looked me in the eye and said, 'You know the antisemitism you warned me about – it's even worse than you feared.'

My firstborn has always been an old soul. At age eight, he distanced himself from a group of boys at school, telling me that they were not nice to each other. My son questioned why anyone would be mean to a friend. As he grew up, I had countless calls from parents thanking me for his kindness. He would stand up for children who were socially awkward and help the neurodiverse child in his class with their homework. That's not to say he was perfect – as a teenager, he gave us his fair share of troubles. But he always studied hard at school and was determined to do the best he possibly could. Like I said, an old soul. But of course, there were so many ways he was still young, still innocent.

His innocence was about to be tested. As the academic year progressed, through the media, we were assured by Vice-Chancellor Mark Scott that there was nothing antisemitic about people interrupting lectures to call for the boycotting of Israel, a country where Jewish students, like my son, had family members in bomb shelters or displaced from their homes. There was nothing antisemitic, we were told, about calls to 'Globalise the Intifada', even though my son knew too well that, during the Second Intifada, I narrowly avoided being killed in Tel Aviv, when the bus I had missed was blown up by a suicide bomber. Apparently, there was also nothing antisemitic about posters plastered on campus encouraging people to discover 'The Real Hamas' – the same 'freedom fighters' who just happened to butcher, rape and kidnap 'settlers from a colonial enterprise'.

I watched in awe as my nineteen-year-old navigated his way through that first year. He would not be silenced. He tried to talk to those with opposing views, even when they threatened to beat him up, donning their keffiyehs as skirts (which in bygone years would have been regarded as cultural appropriation). On Purim, he tried to share hamantaschen cookies with protestors who welcomed his view that the settlers in the West Bank were an impediment to peace, but were not prepared to condemn October 7 as a terrorist attack. My son said that there could only be peace with concessions and dialogue, they said there could only be peace without a Jewish state. And still, he came home and reported that the protestors were nice people, just brainwashed.

Throughout the academic year, my son wrote almost weekly to Mark Scott, expressing his concerns about the antisemitic activity on campus. He earnestly believed that the administration would act to protect Jewish students and remove the encampment, even though he never received a response – not to a single one of his emails. He also questioned the security guards on campus as to why he, a fee-paying student, could not access certain areas of the university during the protests, but the protestors could. He was told that although the protests were peaceful, it was for his own safety. Of course, there was nothing antisemitic here. Nothing at all.

I cautioned my son against visiting the encampment, but he felt the need to bear witness to what was being said at those gatherings. He went there almost daily, albeit without his Jewish jewellery. I accompanied him one day and watched him stand toe-to-toe with a protestor. My heart swelled with pride when he agreed to a debate, on the condition that it be respectful. He held his ground when the protestor yelled in his face that the Nazis colluded with Israel to create the Holocaust. I seethed, but my son put his hand on my shoulder and calmly asked how that was possible when Israel did not exist until 1948. In response, the protestor lunged at him with a two-metre pole holding a Palestinian flag. Thankfully, the protester was tackled by security guards and dragged down.

My son wasn't deterred. He implored Mark Scott, to no avail, to investigate the presence of older men on campus, parading what seemed to be ISIS flags whilst chanting 'Allahu Akhbar'. We later learnt these were not students, but members of Hizb ut-Tahrir, an Islamic fundamentalist organisation. He then wrote a submission for the proposed judicial inquiry, from which I learned that a friend he made in the early weeks of university stopped talking to him once they realised my son was Jewish. Of course, this wasn't antisemitic – how can one expect to be friends with a 'genocidal baby killer'?

My son also presented a modified version of his submission to the Bruce Hodgkinson External Review at The University of Sydney. Having received news that the enquiry was completed, I eagerly told him to check his emails. He said he didn't need to because he knew what it would say: 'Yes, there has been some antisemitism. Not as bad as what you think. But adequate measures have been put in place to address it.' And, in a nutshell, he was right. That was the moment I realised that my child's innocence was lost. He could now see clearly how morally bereft the system at his university is.[1]

*

Lately, each morning, I've been reflecting on my grandfather's decision to escape Germany after watching Hitler refuse to shake hands with gold medallist Jesse Owens. He left his parents behind, unconvinced by their sense of security, the claim that they had 'fought for the Kaiser, and that nothing too terrible will happen to the Jews of Germany'.

And then he left South Africa after the Sharpeville massacre, knowing intrinsically that a country underpinned by racism was not a place to raise a family. As I watch my son head out the door each morning to attend his lectures, I wonder if it's time to leave this country.

Each week my husband and I weigh up our options – where would we move if the climate in Australia becomes even less bearable? For me the answer is easy. There is only one home for us, even if it is a country currently under attack on so many fronts. But he is more cynical; he thinks the Jews need to be spread throughout the diaspora because otherwise Iran will press the button to obliterate us all. As for my son, despite being at the coalface of antisemitism, he continues to genuinely believe that the average Australian is a good person and that, as long as we continue to stand tall and speak up, there is a future for Jews in this country. Unlike his innocence, his optimism persists.

---

1   Isobel Roe, 'University of Sydney vice-chancellor Mark Scott apologises to Jewish students over Students for Palestine encampment', *ABC News*, 19 September 2024.

OPEN HIDING

DANI VALENT

My brother spoke at a Child Survivors of the Holocaust gathering in Melbourne in October 2024. 'Some families suffer from intergenerational trauma,' he said. 'Our family is not one of those.' My father – a child survivor, now 86 – was there. He reached for my brother's hand when he finished speaking. My brother's existence, eloquence and especially his happiness are among the many victories of my father's survival.

My niece spoke next, my sister's older daughter, now fourteen. When she was nine, she travelled with her parents and grandparents to Bratislava and Budapest to visit the sites of her grandfather's Holocaust-shadowed childhood. The cellar he sheltered in. The street corner where his parents were captured and taken away. The apartment where he lived in open hiding, as a Christian. 'I didn't know what "open hiding" meant,' said my niece. 'But I am starting to understand it more.'

So am I.

Since October 7, I have worn a Star of David necklace and hidden it under my top. I have worn a Star of David and touched it most minutes, pressing it against my heart. I have taken off my Star of David because I'm going out. I have taken off my Star of David because I might not remember to keep it hidden. I have left my Star of David at home because I'm scared.

I used to feel the same as my brother: we did not suffer intergenerational trauma. But I have realised it was waiting in my blood. My cells seized with it and they have not eased. The rhetoric around the Hamas attacks and the Israeli response has been like screams in my face, footfalls chasing me from behind, when the only conversations I can have are quiet and horrified. The dialogues clatter in black and white when all I see is grey: complexity writ upon old, old stories that don't slot into glib binaries, facile slogans or meme metrics. Over and over again, I develop answers to questions that no one asks, positions that are subtle but unimpeachable and endlessly rehearsed. I feel responsible, like I will be held to account. I practise vigilance, my skin awake, veins twanging, voice shrinking.

This is the hiding. I have words to say but no courage or breath to say them. I have stories to tell but no faith that hearts are open and listening. As a writer, it is a strange feeling to be silenced by the notion that communicating is pointless. There is this feeling of waiting for it to go away – to go back, to go forward? But if I have learnt anything it is that 'away' just means within – and what is 'it' anyway? My father told me early on in all this that I did not have to speak or solve. 'We survived by staying quiet,' he said.

I don't consider myself a quiet person. As a restaurant critic and freelance food journalist with a podcast and a public profile, my trade is in opinion. It is not my habit to throw my thoughts around lightly. Rather, I gather them carefully, plait them slowly, logic bound to lexicon. I try to be accurate and contextual, leaning on the moral protection – and indeed the legal excuse – of truthfulness and facts. But they are an insufficient shield in these times.

The week before October 7, I visited an Israeli restaurant in my neighbourhood with the aim of reviewing it. I loved the place – the herb oil slashed into tahini; lamb in juicy, salty strands pushed into golden-fried pita; barramundi baked in a rich, spicy tomato sauce; the Friday challah and candles – but I held back on publishing. It was not the right time. I thought about slotting in the story months later. Every month actually. No, not now, they might get harassed, not yet and not yet. I berate myself for a lack of courage. I tell myself it's fine to stay quiet. I am brave, I am scared, I touch my Star of David and put my computer away. It's my choice how I allow myself to be drained. Should I review that new Palestinian food truck? Is food still communion, a site of sharing and exchange?

I remember my own trip to Europe with my father when I was 21. We went to his childhood sites of near misses and disaster, surveying them like anthropologists, distant at times, plunged into horror at others. Budapest, where Jews were shot into the river making it run red. We watched the water rushing by, then walked to eat cake. Auschwitz, choking with ghosts. Leaving the concentration camp, I offered to drive and sent the car almost immediately over a kerb, lurching, my eyes blurred, banal danger layered over vast historical peril.

We drove to the old family farm in Slovakia where my father spent happy summers before the war, then was hidden for six terrifying weeks in 1944. In one field, an ancient peasant couple emerged from a dim, low-roofed cottage. My father spoke to them in halting Slovak and, like a dawn breaking, they slowly recognised the small child returned, their stiff clothes bending like boards as they held their hands to their faces, the gentle surprise of the unshockable. My father took me to a corn field, the leaves whispering, the sun steely behind grey clouds in the late afternoon. 'I used to do this when I was little,' he told me, then pushed between the corn plants and crouched down so he was hidden, a man playing at being a boy. He was lost to me for moments, everything breathing, then the sun found a way through the grey, the corn a sudden green and golden shimmer. My father stood up, no longer hidden. 'I am here!'

WRITING IN THE TIME OF WAR

LEE KOFMAN

Just before October 7, I began clearing my decks – which I always do before embarking on writing a new book. This cleansing ritual, both practical and symbolic, can take weeks. The goal is to declutter my life and mind, to create a comfortable space for my muses to lounge about in their silk negligées. I unsubscribe from group emails, restock my pantry, submit tax returns, prepare my writing classes in advance.

The plan was to make a start on two works – a novel and a memoir that have lived in my head for many years – and to see which, if any, would take root. It was to be the first time in eight years that I'd write without a contract, with no deadlines, and I both dreaded and desired this freedom. To warm up my writing muscles, which had atrophied during the preceding months while I was focused on promoting my latest book, I planned to start with some writing exercises and taking 'contemplative walks'. I was keen to begin, to swap my public speaker's uniform of fancy dresses for tracksuits, to resume the externally quieter and internally wilder existence of a writer. The start date shone bright in my diary. Then, unspeakable horrors struck my former country, where I lived for fourteen years, until my mid-twenties. Then, the destruction in Gaza began. Then everything – everything – in my partly uncluttered, mostly fulfilling life changed… And I could no longer write.

***

In my early thirties, I experienced a lengthy writer's block. During those four years, I wrote for as many hours as I usually did. I even produced some publishable short works. But I hated everything I wrote, and most of what I started I never finished – I lost faith in my writing abilities. And I was confused about what I should write. I was trying to please an imagined audience instead of expressing what felt urgent – wounds and failures and uncomfortable desires, all that fire…

As 2023 drew to its terrible end, as far as writing was concerned, I wasn't confused. I had faith in my projects; I even had the voice for them, I felt. I wasn't blocked. Rather, I was experiencing something I hadn't yet experienced in my passionately bookish life, which began when I learned to read at the age of four. Words were my life. Yet, now, I had lost faith in words. Or rather, I had lost faith in their worth.

The tipping point wasn't the barbarism of Hamas and the suffering of Palestinians. I could write in the face of these atrocities, could hope that my writing – anyone's writing – might infuse the darkening world with some light, some goodness. I had always believed this – that, with some exceptions of course, literature equals goodness. That it affords us oases in which to recuperate as well as encourages empathy and reflection. But the response to the October 7 massacre and the ensuing outbreak of antisemitism from Australia's hyper-educated, progressive elites, including many writers I'd known and respected for years, writers whose books fill the shelves of my study, quashed this belief.

In the immediate aftermath of the massacre, I received supportive messages from many peers in private. Yet public expressions of concern for the Israeli victims were thin on the ground. Soon, the silence at best, and the mental gymnastics to justify what happened on October 7 at worst, became the modus operandi in the arts world. It was a mindfuck to realise that people who live and breathe words, and arrange them in ways that make me feel stuff, could be so selective about suffering.

Things grew worse, fast. More than a few writers – authors of nuanced, thoughtful books, people known for their compassion – rushed to take sides in an ancient, endlessly complex conflict that even I, someone who spent her youth in Israel and has written books in its language, cannot properly grasp. The dominant conversations in my milieu weren't about peace, about bringing people together. Instead, fiercely anti-Israel open letters appeared, signed by significant numbers of the Australian literati. In those letters as well as on socials, words like 'apartheid' and 'white-settler-colonial state' were being automatically, and ignorantly, applied to my former country by people whose life's work has been to take care with language. Rather than interrogating their knowledge of history and sources of information about the unfolding Israel-Hamas war, my peers seemed more concerned with conforming to the trending demonisation of Israel and 'Zionists' – meaning Jews who affirm Israel's right to exist. Meaning nearly 80 percent of Australian Jews according to conservative estimates.[1] Meaning also many Jews like me, who still believe in a two-state solution, who ache for both sides…

Watching the Australian literary world become obsessed with one foreign conflict while many others, often bloodier – Sudan's civil war and the Russia-Ukraine war to mention a few – unfolded around the globe, felt not only deeply disheartening but deeply personal. In my youth, I travelled regularly to open-air music festivals, a rite of passage for young Israelis. I'd get drunk on the music coming from everywhere, weave colourful beads into my messy locks and, in the early hours of morning, happily doze off on a sleeping bag spread on the grass damp with dew and beer. After several such pulsing days I'd come home dirty, exhausted and deeply alive, and begin saving for the next festival.

It wasn't difficult to imagine that it could have been me being butchered at the Nova festival. And here were writers whose books and conversations I cherished, writing students I nurtured, people with whom I thought I shared something fundamental and visceral, who – I now knew – could flippantly dismiss my life with a catchy Instagram post from the comfort of their home, which nobody was planning to burn. The membrane between my skin and my peers' political stances grew thin.

This membrane utterly vanished as antisemitism spread its tentacles all over Australia. Few people from my milieu seemed concerned that Jewish people were now being targeted in this country in countless ways. It felt even more surreal to see some well-known Australian authors expressing explicitly antisemitic views and getting away with it.

And so it was. I lost faith in writing because I lost faith in writers. Everywhere I looked, instead of thoughtfulness I saw conformism and virtue signalling, and at the expense of my blood. That is what it felt like. That is what it still feels like.

So what was the point of writing?

***

It was not, however, as simple as that: October 7 happened and my literary dream collapsed. It was more that the tragedy, and the ensuing war, brought to light the dark, slimy things that I, eager to belong, had been trying to ignore for years; things that had made me increasingly uncomfortable among my literary tribe – a tribe at whose gatherings I was often the only Jew and always the sole Israeli. To my knowledge, I am the only Israeli-Australian author with some sort of a public profile and, as such, my belonging has always felt tentative.

All those cracks that I tried to ignore – such as the literary event where I signed my book for another writer, remarking that her Egyptian name reminded me of the Hebrew word for 'lake'. Her pleasant demeanour abruptly changed and she said she wanted 'nothing to do with Israel'. That incident disturbed me more than it possibly should have, as in my youth I often holidayed in the Sinai Peninsula, sharing joints with Egyptians.

It took many more similar incidents, so-called micro-aggressions, for my barometer to become attuned to the antisemitic undercurrents humming in my tribe's depths. I'm particularly thinking of the occasion when I met an internationally renowned author who immediately informed me, unprompted, that he would not travel to Israel until the occupation ends. As we kept talking, it became clear that his political principles didn't stop him from visiting many countries with questionable regimes, including Russia, my country of birth.

This encounter prompted me to finally acknowledge how crucial my Russian origins had been to my acceptance in the Australian literary community, where Israel is seen as the geographical location of humanity's demonic elements. This was the part of me that saved the day. Forget gulags, murdered journalists, annexed satellite states – as my books were published in Australia, the romance of birches and Chekhov swirled around me in every interview and literary get-together. I remember how during one interview on ABC Radio, despite repeatedly telling the interviewer that my writing life began in Hebrew, he kept insisting on discussing my change of writing languages from Russian to English.

To allow a writer like myself, with a powerful (albeit complex) connection to Israel, to speak about it hasn't been the thing to do since way before October 7. No matter that I oppose settlements and support Palestinian rights, still I pose a risk to the cozy literary consensus that Israel can do no right. The one short story I wrote in English that loosely engages with the Israeli-Palestinian conflict, without demonising either side, got rejected from most Australian literary magazines. (Eventually it found a home in *Griffith Review*.)

In perhaps the most striking example, when the scandal around Elizabeth Gilbert's novel set in Siberia erupted, I was approached by the media to comment – despite having left Russia when I was twelve. In contrast, on the literary festival circuit I've never been invited to panels where Israel is concerned. I am not a political writer, but neither are many other speakers on such panels. I, at least, did my time in a sealed room during the Gulf War and in compulsory army service... But nobody has ever wanted to hear what I have to say about the place where I spent my formative years. Just as these days, when calls to boycott Israeli writers and books proliferate to much publicity, no journalist has ever solicited an opinion from me.

So this is what I'd been trying to ignore all these years – that I could attend the literary party where everyone is vigorously encouraged by publishers, funding bodies and peers to 'go to their roots', but only so long as I expose my Russian roots and leave the Israeli ones to rot.

***

You know the poem, 'First They Came'? Well, first they came for Israeli writers and now, since October 7 brought to the boil all the simmering hatreds, the literary world has become antagonistic to any writer who happens to be Jewish (unless they are publicly anti-Zionist), even if they've never written or spoken about Israel. 'Is this writer Jewish?' goes the refrain. 'So where do they stand on the Palestine question?' (Can you imagine a Chinese-Australian author being asked to declare their stance on Uyghurs?) And, increasingly, it's far more blunt: 'Jewish? Then let's shut them up.'

Over the last year, not a few Jewish writers I know told me, as well as the media, how professional gatekeepers – publishers, literary agents, grant assessors, festival organisers, booksellers – made it clear to them that now is not the time for Jewish stories.[2] Jewish writers are effectively being cancelled, including literally cancelled, as has happened with some of my organised events too. Several Australian literary journals have now made it their policy to not publish 'Zionists', which rules out most Jews.

Nowadays, I suspect, I am being doubly ruled out. Since October 7, I have discarded my romantic Russian persona and come out as my full self: a Russian-Ukrainian-Israeli-Australian Jew. A Jewy Jew. A contrary Jew. In November 2023, along with several other Jewish writers, I organised an open letter signed by almost 1500 Jews and allies, urging our creative and academic peers to call out antisemitism. It was either that or sink into depression. I had to act, even if it seemed futile against the tsunami of Jew-hatred and disinformation.

I spoke about the letter in the national and international media, outing myself. But I was also outed against my will in the famous doxxing of a WhatsApp group for Australian Jewish creatives and academics that I established for mutual support and self-preservation (which later led to new anti-doxxing legislation). I was called a 'genocidal Zionist' and accused of various fantastical crimes, including working for the Mossad. After that, I lost any chance I had of passing as the 'inoffensive Russian writer' and some of the prominent literary organisations with whom I'd worked closely for years stopped inviting me to teach, interview authors or assess writing awards. Some writers I've known well unfollowed me on social media, and would probably snub me in real life too – although I have yet to test this as these days I no longer feel as safe as I used to at literary events and so I haven't attended as many as I normally would. I also feel anxious during my public speaking gigs, and even when I occasionally use (never political) texts by Israeli writers in my teaching. My identity is an easy target and, as in a schoolyard where bullies outnumber their prey, in the literary yard the numbers have never been in my favour. I now live my writing life on high alert.

***

Several years ago, I curated an anthology of personal essays called *Split: True stories of leaving, loss and new beginnings*. My introductory essay was a passionate plea against fetishising redemptive endings. Not everything can be redeemed, I argued, and writing must reflect life, not photoshop it. I still believe this, but as I'm weaving this dark tale, I must tell you that it does contain some (albeit crooked) redemption.

Seven months after October 7 I resumed writing.

I resumed writing even though, professionally speaking, I no longer know what the future holds for me. I might be writing into the void. Paradoxically, it is this uncertainty that has inspired me again.

Both books I was planning to write were explorations of my Jewishness, including my Israeli-ness. I felt an urgency to write about this intrinsic part of myself and also I felt anxiety. Before the war, I kept calculating how far I could take this writing without killing my publication prospects. But now that the publishing industry is openly hostile to people like me, in some way I feel liberated. I have little to lose, so I feel freer than I've felt in my 25 years in Australia to be myself on the page. And this counts for something, right?

I wonder if this is how dissident writers in the Soviet Union felt. I am particularly thinking of Mikhail Bulgakov, the author of my favourite novel, *The Master and Margarita* – a biting critique of Stalin's regime. Bulgakov, who lived under Stalin, burnt the novel's early version because he thought nobody would publish it (indeed, during his lifetime nobody did). Still, he restarted and finished his masterpiece. Nowadays, one of its most quoted lines is: 'Manuscripts don't burn.'

I am no Bulgakov. I have no illusions about my talent, nor do I share his belief that my writing will matter in the long term. Yet I feel that it matters *right* now, when the overwhelming majority of Jewish voices are being viewed as dissident and are being suppressed. *Now*, when Israelis, as well as any Jews who are not openly anti-Zionist, are continuously dehumanised. Precisely now is the time for stories like mine – to re-humanise ourselves when nobody else will. We cannot afford to burn our manuscripts, even if nobody wants or dares to publish them. This is why I write again. And out of defiance too.

---

1   Andrew Markus, Crossroads23: Surveying Australian Jews on Israel, *Plus 61J*, 14 June 2023.
2   Jessica Abelsohn, 'Silenced: the battle of Jewish creatives', *Australian Jewish News*, 29 November 2024.

BOILED EGGS

RUBY KRANER-TUCCI

My grandmother is yelling at me. It's April 2023 and we're at a Passover Seder at Gary Smorgon House, the Jewish aged care facility she calls home. My grandmother is sitting to my left. She yells again, louder. A few residents pipe up. 'Shush,' they snap in a tone reserved exclusively for old people. My grandmother yells a lot, apparently.

'I won't tell anyone,' she says, looking right into my eyes.

On this special occasion in the Jewish calendar, the table is set beautifully: a patterned tablecloth, polished silver cutlery, a vase of red roses. A customary Seder plate – a symbolic centrepiece filled with meaning and tradition – sits in the middle and on it, a shiny, perfectly shelled, boiled egg. An egg drenched in water salty like the tears of my Jewish ancestors. An egg my grandmother desperately wants to eat.

'You can't eat that one, it's for decoration,' I whisper. I'm laughing, I can't help it.

My grandmother bangs her fist on the table. The rabbi stops

his sermon, not that anyone was listening anyway, and casts us a frustrated glare. Opposite me, my aunt and uncle look up from the phones they're hiding under the table. To my right, my mother mouths an apology. The only person unphased is Ruth, the 101-year-old who was lucky enough to be placed with my family for Passover. She smiles sweetly as my face turns red.

I appease my grandmother: 'They'll bring out the real eggs soon, the eggs you're allowed to eat. Once the rabbi finishes.'

But who am I, really, to deny my grandmother a boiled egg? My 93-year-old grandmother who narrowly missed following her own mother, two sisters and countless other relatives to the Treblinka extermination camp. My grandmother, who can speak six languages, who migrated and assimilated in Israel then Australia, and worked her whole life to provide for her family. Isn't a boiled egg the least I can offer her?

In a flash, I stick my fork in the egg and place it on my grandmother's plate. The egg is gone so quickly I barely see my grandmother chew. I only know she's eaten it because of the coughing fit that follows. The rabbi perseveres. I'm still laughing.

Six months later, it's October 7.

I was in England on an extended holiday when Hamas terrorists stormed southern Israel to massacre, mutilate, rape and kidnap whoever they could find.

I was at a park with my boyfriend in Shakespeare's country when the Jewish world experienced its largest loss of life in a single day since the Holocaust.

I was *playing* on the fucking playground.

When my phone pinged with the news, I immediately thought

of my grandmother. I wanted to be with her, to cry with her, to let her hold me.

I wanted to buy a dozen eggs, drown them in salt water and stuff my face with them.

By the time I returned home, my grandmother's dementia had firmly set in. She no longer recognised me, but she was happy to spend time in my company. Together, we ate month-old Tim Tams and watched '90s sitcoms. I listened as she repeated the same stories.

'I kissed the ground when the plane landed,' my grandmother said. I knew this one by heart. 'I got down on my hands and my knees and I kissed the tarmac in Israel.'

I nodded along, feigning the interest my family's migration story so desperately deserved. A story spanning Russia, Poland, France, Israel and Australia. A story of pain and resilience.

'Do you understand? I actually *kissed* it. I was home.'

It wasn't long before my grandmother reverted to her mother tongue, Yiddish. The language that her children couldn't fully understand. The language she used for telling secrets. English wasn't even on the agenda. Our relationship was reduced to warm smiles.

Six months after October 7, my grandmother died.

A large part of me is thankful she wasn't able to truly understand how much the world has changed. Would seeing such brutality strike the country where she rebuilt her life post-World War II, met her husband – a union that lasted over 60 years – and had her first daughter, have triggered her own trauma?

An even larger part of me is thankful my grandmother wasn't able to see the antisemitism in Australia that followed and has only continued to escalate. My brother's friend being denied a seat by other students at his university's law ball because he wore a kippah. My Jewish colleagues being doxxed, Jewish businesses being boycotted, the 'Jew die' graffiti that was plastered across a local Jewish school.

Most of all, I'm glad my grandmother isn't here to witness the pain of my family. My aunt's voice breaking while discussing the hostages captive in Gaza, holding her granddaughter close during Chanukah celebrations. My mother bursting into tears at police warning Jews to stay away from the city – my hometown – because our safety can't be guaranteed. My non-Jewish, Italian father – my guide who always has the answers – solemnly telling me, 'I don't know how to protect you. I don't know what to do.'

I don't easily pass the 'Jew test'. I didn't attend a Jewish school or youth group. I don't speak Hebrew or Yiddish. I live a few suburbs away from Melbourne's Bagel Belt, and I celebrate Christmas and Easter.

Growing up, I relished my Jewish identity. With the unwavering support of my father, my mother imparted the value of Judaism in my life. For most in our circle, we were 'the Jewish family' – the only Jewish family they knew – and I never thought that to be a bad thing. We taught our friends how to play dreidel. We introduced them to challah. We threw epic Purim parties. We explained why gefilte fish wasn't really that bad. We were the fun Jews, the exotic Jews.

I always loved being the centre of attention in this way, but as I grew older and my social circles expanded, I started to self-censor. When I met someone new and revealed my heritage, I would often notice the second-too-long pauses. The darting eyes. The clearing of throats. Sometimes there was a polite nod, rarely were there questions. People were always more interested in my Italian background. So, when a friend made an off-the-cuff Jewish joke, it felt easier to laugh along than to defend myself. When I was told my new haircut made me look 'more Jewish', I smiled politely to keep the peace. When my brother was playfully called a 'Jew dog' by his mate, I stayed quiet. These instances were too sporadic to impact me. It wasn't a big deal.

That was until October 7.

The flooding of Instagram came first. Each scroll through my friends' virtual lives brought vicious anti-Israel sentiment. Slogans calling for the eradication of Israel, the land that kept my family safe: *From the River to the Sea*. Slogans I couldn't help but see as personal attacks: *Don't Wash your Holocaust Trauma with Palestinian Blood*. Why didn't they speak to me, possibly their only Jewish friend, before they spoke out online? Did they think about me at all?

I prepared myself for the debate and discussion that were sure to come. For my friends to ask about my views on the war and share their own. But it didn't come. It has never come. No one has been curious about my perspective on Netanyahu. No one has seemed worried about my family in Israel.

But I'm the fun Jew so I say nothing.

I self-censor.

I bottle it up.

Instead of speaking out, I deleted the app. As someone part of a generation that uses social media to connect, I was now left completely out of the loop. I missed birthdays, engagement announcements and the welcoming of new babies.

I deleted the app, yet I couldn't escape it – this obsession with the Gaza war, as if there were no other large scale, deadly conflicts unfolding around the world. At work, my colleagues and I received death threats. *Jew, two-faced bastards, burn in hell*. Everyone said it came with the territory. The territory of working in Jewish media. *You deserve to be teleported into a Palestinian 'safe zone' moments before the bombs hit.* But I'm still working in Australia. I'm still Australian. *All you fucking Jews will die.*

It's a week after the one-year anniversary of October 7 and I'm at a Chinese restaurant with two non-Jewish friends eating cheap dumplings.

'How's work for you?' One friend asks me, after they've both spoken at length about their jobs and boyfriends and travel plans and parents and latest TV obsessions.

'We just received another death threat. It was so bad we called the police,' I say, ignoring the way they shift in their chairs. I don't usually talk about this topic with these friends I've known since high school. This topic of being Jewish.

'Honestly, I've worked at Jewish organisations before, I'm used to the security guards out front and the need to keep our address confidential, but I've never experienced this level of racism,' I continue, hoping to get some recognition, some validation. They exchange a look. One friend tries to speak but nothing comes out.

'I didn't know Australia could be like this. I thought our generation had gotten past antisemitism.' I can't help myself. The burden is getting too heavy, and I want these friends to carry some of the load. 'Maybe I could have handled this year, the mourning of my grandmother, if I was on solid ground, but I'm not. I'm terrified. I practically begged my family to stay home on the October 7 anniversary because I was convinced something bad would happen.'

Still nothing. The clatter of the Chinese restaurant around us helps to fill the silence. My friends look scared, but I can't stop. I *won't* stop.

'I've unfollowed so many people on Instagram, people I've known my whole life, and I don't even know if I disagree with them. That's the thing, I don't know what I believe. I know I'm anti-war and it's horrific seeing Palestinians die, but I also care deeply about a Jewish homeland. You know what really hurts? No one has asked me if I'm okay. No one checks in with me because they've already assumed that because I'm Jewish, they know what I think and they're holding it against me. I've even stopped telling people where I work. I'm so worried that they will judge my decision to work in Jewish media right now. And if I do tell them, I then feel the need to explain it is a progressive organisation that can be critical of Israel, so I can be accepted. And who is even helping us? The police just tell Jews to stay at home, and the government isn't acting fast enough. I used to vote for the Greens, but I can't anymore because they refuse to condemn Hamas, and I can't vote Liberal because combatting antisemitism is the only policy I actually agree with them on. But don't we all want to combat antisemitism? Are people our age really anti-Jewish?'

I catch my breath.

My friends are stunned. They look at each other. I feel a hand on my shoulder. And still, no one speaks. Dead silence from my friends of over a decade.

'Maybe we should just change the topic,' I offer, crushed.

I stifle my tears in our shared Uber home and seek comfort from my fridge. I find a carton of eggs. I boil two and cry. Salty tears, like those of my ancestors.

WALLS

KYLIE MOORE-GILBERT

Without really knowing it, I had spent the three years before October 7 putting up walls. Somehow, this world which I had been thrust back into, my so-called 'real life' was too lurid, too sonorous, too discombobulating. I needed to keep it at bay. There was such a thing as too much freedom, or so I felt. I needed defences.

As a former prisoner of the Iranian regime, the irony of this wasn't lost on me. All those long and pointless days spent staring at physical walls – knowing their every crack and crevice, every swirl of their faux-marble tile, every stain and smear. Longing for the world I imagined outside, a world of rapidly retreating memories. But the moment I finally arrived there, I began to beat my retreat. I started erecting walls of the mental kind. There is comfort in building oneself a fortress, there is security in fencing in those parts of yourself which might shatter.

I had buttressed my fragility with illusions of stoicism and resilience, convincing myself that I was healed. I went about my daily life and tried to put all thoughts of back there, of Iran and the Middle

East, and all it had given and taken away, firmly out of my head. I found a non-Jewish partner whose own background allowed him to understand what I had survived when so many others could not. I had a child. I rejoined academia. The walls were there, but if I felt them at all I would say they were a soothing presence, more guardrail than razor wire.

Then, suddenly, the flood. Families herded together in their pyjamas. Young people frantic and zig-zagging through the desert. The pockmarked streets of Sderot. The unspeakable fate of too many children on both sides of the border fence.

As I clutched my own child tightly to my chest, I felt tremors. For me it had all been too bright; an endless, sickening, 24-hour LED brightness. But for them there was no light at all. Where I had shivered in the winter chill that descended from the Zagros mountains, there they were sticky and humid and choking. Desperate for oxygen, struggling to breathe, the smell of soil all around them. Was it a damp kind of soil, or was it sandy, or dusty? What sort of mental games did they play to pass the time, to blunt their fears? Did their narrow, bunker-like walls give them a perverse sense of comfort, as 'real life' twisted and shrunk and retreated with time? When they came out (if they came out), would they too build a fortress of the mind, and would that too come crashing down in the wake of some future unspeakable horror?

As someone who lived among Islamist radicals for years, I recognised the vocabulary of these fighters as they raped and tortured and murdered, on a visceral, instinctive level. They saw the world in the same way my interrogators had. Explained it away, justified it, revelled in it. Indeed, my captors were the ones bankrolling their depravity.

The horrors of that day replayed in an endless loop in my mind. Images, real or envisioned, filtered into my subconscious, as I scrambled to delete, to log out, to suspend all comments. They merged with my own memories, growing in colour and sharpness and focus. Jail cells and bound hands and blindfolds and faraway screams and solitary confinement and beatings by guards and curse the Jews and we will destroy Israel and in fifteen years we will be praying at Al Aqsa…

In the streets of my city were IRGC flags and insignia. A fist raised, a globe conquered, an Arabic phrase from *Surat al-Anfal* – the verse of the spoils of war. A handful of so-called friends called to sound out where I stood on 'the genocide.' When I refused to throw myself headfirst into the rapidly swelling tide, rising seemingly out of nowhere at bewildering speed, I was dropped and denounced and smeared. Losing my liberty to years of psychological torture and physical abuse no longer cut it. Now it seems I was required to adopt the same ideological positions as my own captors.

Suddenly, I was putting up walls again. Scaffolding to safeguard against the soul-crushing pain of that day. Barriers to hold back my grief at the devastation wrought afterwards. October 7 was a dam breaking, an earth cracking, a seismic shuddering. It was letting too much flow inwards too quickly. It was drowning in one's own ballast water, it was trying to swim towards the light whilst raking one's hands along the ocean floor. I needed to shut it out, to fence it off.

But, as I scrambled to re-erect my defences, I couldn't quite block out a furtive little voice, whispering shrilly, sometimes in Persian: *On October 6 they, too, thought that walls would protect them.*

THE PAIN OF OTHERS

LYNETTE CHAZAN

Everyone asks where you were on October 7. I was at a psychiatry conference in the Broadbeach Sofitel. It was the end of a day of learning and mingling, more mingling than learning. Slouching back on the cool sheets of a king size bed, I saw it on CNN. It was beyond imagination: the rupture of the Gaza fence in a hundred places; an army of men on motorbikes, hang-gliders and pick-up trucks flooding the south, hunting for people to kill, rape, kidnap, the numbers mounting by the hour; the dawning realisation there were others on every border that might join at any moment; the Israel Defense Forces nowhere.

It could have been us. It *was* us, or at least our parents and grandparents. But there I was, in my elegant hotel room, without walls or even flimsy drapes, psychically naked, in a state of shock.

When I stumbled back to the conference the next morning, I saw people for whom this was another news item. For me, it was the world falling apart.

The day after, at work, there was silence from my colleagues – people who usually enquire after others' wellbeing when, say, there is a cancer scare, or a divorce. Colleagues I have supported in times of crisis, who know I have loved ones in Israel and have travelled there often. The silence had heft, substance. It was as if I were sleepwalking, cut off from the life all around. And then, equally shocking: a patient crossed the room before leaving my consulting room and hugged me.

Two days later, before the bruising had even begun to set in, the Sydney Opera House was lit up in blue and white. It was a deep consolation, this solidarity. But crowds gathered there, bellowing 'Allahu Akhbar'. Did they also shout, 'Gas the Jews!' or 'Where are the Jews?', as some passionately debated in the media? Does it matter? They were looking for Jews. The Jews were not there. The Jews had been warned away by the police. A lone Jewish man with an Israeli flag was the only one arrested.

It has taken months for this to sink in: those people were *celebrating*.

On October 13, my professional organisation, the College of Psychiatrists, sent out a sympathy message for Gaza – but not for Israel.[1]

There was no *I'll ride with you*.[2]

We had hardly begun mourning when we started to hear it didn't happen; it was all a Zionist fabrication. Despite the video and witness accounts of dead women with torn clothes, open legs and damaged genitals at the Nova festival site,[3][4] the 'believe all women' crowd said there was no evidence of rape. Had I heard all of this before – the cataclysm and its almost simultaneous denial – somewhere in another life?

I could not find my bearings.

***

I am a woman – my neurobiology is tuned to a baby's whimper. I am a psychiatrist – I attend to human darkness and pain. I am a Jew – I am tied to Israel through history, genetics, religion, myth, fear, memory and yearning; and I am immersed in centuries of Talmudic devotion to debate, justice and mercy. I am a Diaspora Jew – my custom of accommodation is what Sigmund Freud prescribed as 'a little necessary masochism'.

All in all, the pain of others weighs heavily on me. You could even say I specialise in the pain of others.

***

Every morning since October 7, I wake and scroll through the news. The devastation is unspeakable: pictures of Gazan fathers stumbling through rubble carrying dead babies, entire neighbourhoods crushed into dust. I scroll faster, looking for something to relieve the pain, but instead find a photo of a fallen Israeli soldier, smiling. It is the sort of photo parents joyfully pull out to show their friends, the sort I have of my three adult sons. It *could* have been them had Australia not accepted my family after the war. In these moments, every bone wants to cry out for a ceasefire.

Many military experts say the Israel-Hamas war has the lowest civilian to combatant ratio ever achieved in urban warfare,[5][6] that Israel's war aims – to rescue the hostages and to destroy a terror organisation that vows Israel's destruction – are legitimate. But many NGOs and progressive journalists say this is genocide and hence, by logical extension, that I am a genocide supporter.

The accusation enters at a point of infinite defencelessness. In the diaspora, Jews do the vulnerability Israelis cannot afford. We are used to brandishing pens, not swords, to abhor violence. We drip wine from our little fingers on Passover Seder night to remind ourselves that we must not rejoice in the drowning of the Egyptians in the Red Sea. Our cup must not be full when others suffer.

I make myself imagine being a Palestinian right now: a mother moving her family and belongings yet again, the frantic search for a lost child, the constant deafening explosions. It is too hard; it is like holding my own head underwater. Is there no limit to empathy? All humans on earth are equal; I know this. It is my love that is limited. Am I expected to weep for everyone? I do weep for the Gazan children. I do care. But it is never enough. And that is not good enough. Even our kids say that. 'You should care about everyone equally, Mum.' That's what they say. Is there anyone of whom such empathy is expected?

***

In November, the community of the virtuous line up in judgement of Israel: the United Nations that once meant something inspirational to me, the NGOs I used to admire, the ICC, the Pope. In the media, culpability is measured by body count; Hamas and IDF reports about casualty numbers and their causes are considered equally credible. There is scorn in a newscaster's voice: 'When will this be enough vengeance?' she asks. I try to imagine what I would think if I were not so involved, so Jewish. They want an arms embargo, a one-state solution, an immediate two-state solution, reward the terror, leave Hamas and Hezbollah intact, anything to make the war stop. Ideological positions are batted about like tennis balls. I do not hear a serious discussion about how any of these solutions will impact real people.

The meaning of words I thought I understood is gutted. Multiple dizzying inversions are on repeat. Islamist terrorists are freedom fighters. Jewish refugees from Europe and the Middle East returning to their ancestral homeland are colonisers. Terms associated with the Holocaust – Nazis, concentration camp, ethnic cleansing – have become accusations against the Jewish State. Worst of all is the charge of *genocide*, its meaning diluted beyond recognition, originally coined to describe the systematic murder of six million people like my grandparents – who did not attack anyone, who adored Vienna and never stopped adoring it, and who wanted nothing more than to belong.

In kind circles, it is still permissible to speak of your father's arm tattoo, to join the line of the wretched. But Israel is about politics, isn't it? And politics is something else entirely. Those who defend us say: 'I believe that Israel has a right to exist,' while urbanites in cafés discuss Israel's proposed non-existence in revelatory tones, before moving on to weekend plans. Our existence, it seems, is again up for grabs.

Sometimes, in dark moments, I wonder if Israel's destruction, dressed up in human rights, is the world's clandestine fetish.

***

The animus against Israel spreads to Australian Jews. Attacks on us proliferate. The words 'JEW DIE' appear on the fence of my old school. Holocaust survivors in nursing homes are guarded. Jewish students are kicked out of share houses, writers off literary panels, therapists and patients subtly fire each other. On Etsy, I find mugs inscribed with 'Zionist Tears' for $26.25. Drink up, my friends! Sometimes, when I am not overwhelmed by fear, I marvel at the hate. Its manifestations are growing increasingly bizarre, like zebras appearing in my backyard.

In this shattered world, I am only comfortable in the company of the shattered.

***

Every day I am my own defence attorney, without presumption of innocence. I must prove I am not a monster. Can it really be that everyone is wrong? I don't read novels anymore; I have no room for fiction. Podcasts about the war become an addiction. Each is an antidote: *Call Me Back* by Dan Senor, for ignorance and anguish; *For Heaven's Sake* for moral reckoning; *Democracy Now* and MSNBC for bias. I must know. I must be able to answer difficult questions, to interrogate my anguish and parochialism, to distinguish truth from falsehood. Could I be paranoid? After all, I am a post-Holocaust Jew attuned to the footfall of enemies at night. So, I listen and listen. I think by now I could write an encyclopaedia about the Middle East.

Some Jews, a handful of them but loud, also line up against Israel and their fellow Jews. They see their grandparents' suffering in Palestinian suffering. There are now good Jews and there are 'Zionists'. After spending a lifetime trying to be a decent human being (so many of us want to be 'good' as per *Tikun Olam* – the Jewish imperative to heal the world), I am suddenly in doubt. Because the Nazi extermination project lurks within me – so too lurks the question of whether what comes at me is deserved. The accusation of genocide by association seeps into my soul.

I am easily gaslit.

***

My feelings may amount to nothing – but there they are. I do know others suffer so much more. I still walk about in my comfortable house, earn a comfortable living, my boys are – *Baruch Hashem* – healthy. But Jews have been strong before. They have been strong and demolished many times before.

The extent to which my shaming is justified – my virtue or vileness – is an open question. In the CBD, they call me 'baby-killer', so I keep away from the CBD. The world screams 'Stop the war!' I want it to stop too, but I am afraid that those who vow the destruction of my people, to repeat October 7 'again and again', could indeed realise their vision.

I am no stranger to shame. It stalks my patients, because of events for which they bear little responsibility: childhood abuse, a parent's abandonment, occasionally just for being born. Sometimes it moves slowly through the blood like a parasite, sometimes fast like an incendiary bullet exploding within. I don't tend to see the perpetrators themselves in my rooms. Strangely enough, they tend to be shameless.

I observe my need to defend my own collapsing psyche. I search for my doctor's bag. Shaming, I have come to realise, is a weapon of war no less than rockets. Sometimes I fantasise about forfeiting my 99.8 percent Ashkenazi genes and going off the Jewish grid altogether. Or in the opposite direction – packing up and making *Aliyah*, moving to Israel. For a while, I look only at the media that restores a sense of safety and integrity, like the footage of the rescue of hostages. But it is only for a few hours every day, when I am around my patients and registrars, that I feel like my old self, the one who is regarded as sane and decent.

***

Society's moral compass, the sense of what is good and what is bad, is our spiritual north and south. It is the invisible fabric of our lives. For me, as for many, or perhaps most, Jews, this moral fabric has been ripped apart like the high-tech fence the Israelis also thought was impregnable.

I may be easily gaslit, but some things I do know. Australians would demand massive forces to protect us from those determined to destroy us. Progressives would discover the limits of diplomacy when it came to their own safety. Australians would not accept a ceasefire that leaves terror threats on every border. And the world would not try to stop Australia.

***

I am no genocide supporter. But I now feel myself to be a stranger in my own country. The pain of others weighs heavily, but I turn my back for a moment more. I light the Shabbat candles with my family, I see the light reflecting off their faces. In this war of nerves, everyone seeks innocence. Everyone wants to be right. The cup of virtue, it seems to me, contains the dregs of a cold latte. The cup of pain runs over for everyone.

---

1   The RANZCP issued an amendment a week later after distress was expressed by the membership.
2   Brittany Ruppert, 'Martin Place Siege: #illridewithyou hashtag goes viral', *Sydney Morning Herald*, 15 December 2014.
3   Jeffrey Gettleman, Adam Sella & Anat Schwartz, 'How Hamas weaponised sexual violence on October 7', *The New York Times*, 28 December 2023.
4   'Screams Before Silence', Kastina Communications, 2024.
5   Per Bauhn, 'Just war, human shields, and the 2023–24 Gaza War', *Israel Affairs* 30:5, p.863.
6   John Spencer, 'Israel implemented more measures to prevent civilian casualties than any other nation in history', *Newsweek*, 31 January 2024.

FAITH OVER FEAR

DENA AMY KAPLAN

Today is my 36th birthday, and I just received the greatest gift I could have ever dreamed of. Three of our girls – three hostages – have been returned home. I sob as I think about what they've endured; they are braver than words can express. I will never forget this birthday.

It's hard to believe it's been fifteen months since October 7, another day I will never forget. The initial terror and trauma of witnessing what happened was one thing, but the days and months that followed were the hardest part. Watching my friends and colleagues support the terrorists who murdered and kidnapped our women, children, the elderly and babies, was devastating. Seeing the world, including many of my friends, justify the attacks and twist reality was what has hurt the most. I feel particularly angry at all the urban white Australians who chant in the rallies their support for the 'freedom fighters'.

As a Jew in the public eye – a dancer, musician, actor and music producer – when I spoke up online, I faced abuse, daily. I lost half of my following on Instagram. I lost friends – many of them. I lost work opportunities and my career stalled.

In the first post I shared publicly about October 7, I asked why there was so much silence when it came to Jews, where was the outrage? The backlash was revolting. I received threats, even about my baby daughter, and warnings that 'they would find me'. I deleted the post and my nervous system went into overdrive. I changed the locks on my doors and made sure my agents didn't share my address with anyone, including PR companies. I lived in constant fear. Every time I held my daughter, I couldn't shake the images of the babies who had been killed or kidnapped. I became an unstable and irrational version of myself. The terror I felt was disproportionate to my actual life, but I was in a trauma response. I struggled in therapy, struggled as a new mother, struggled in every other aspect of my life.

Watching antisemitism rise violently in Australia and around the world has felt like history repeating itself. I have found myself asking my sisters: 'Who would hide us if it happened again?' I began to understand, for the first time, how the Holocaust could have occurred. I saw the propaganda machine at work, and the silence and complicity of others. I never imagined that I would feel unsafe in my country and the shadow of antisemitism still haunts me.

Eventually, I deleted social media and banned the news from my home. I had the luxury of doing this, and I don't take that for granted. Choosing to disassociate from this war was a privilege. But I think of the parents of the hostages often. I can't fathom the strength it must take to keep going; holding onto hope is both dangerous and heartbreaking when you're dealing with a terrorist group so cruel that they won't even verify who is alive or dead. And I think about all the Palestinian mothers, with their dead and injured children. All these losses, unfathomable and yet made so real through the continuous stream of media footage.

I also stopped speaking out publicly about Israel and being Jewish because I couldn't handle the emotional toll, and because it was impacting my career. It was no longer safe for me to be Jewish in the public eye – a tragedy, considering how proud I am of my heritage.

When I was first asked to write this essay, I declined. For the same reasons of safety. But today feels different. Three of our girls came back home, and there is a fire inside me once again. I probably won't speak out on social media, as I can't handle the threats from keyboard warriors. But I feel compelled to write this.

***

These days, I find myself wondering whether or not I should send my daughter to a Jewish school. I am proud of my Jewish identity, but I want her to feel safe in this world. I'm not sure that a Jewish school will offer that safety. My nephews attend one of the largest Jewish day schools in Australia, where they have armed security at the doors, and they are no longer permitted to wear their school uniforms, which identify them as Jewish, on excursions. Is this the life I want for my child? Perhaps it's better if she does not identify as Jewish?

Yet, somehow, I always come back to my faith. It's the only way I know to conquer fear – through faith, prayer and turning it over to God. Last year, we had a Hebrew naming ceremony at my synagogue for my daughter. Our brilliant rabbi thanked me for speaking out despite the backlash. I broke down in tears, because by then I already felt silenced and was wondering if I could have done more.

We gave our daughter the Hebrew name Selah, meaning 'to pause and reflect', also known as the 'breath of God'. And as of today, I have had time to pause and reflect on this war, on the antisemitism that has followed, and on my disillusionment with many in Western society and the media. Where I land is this: we, as Jews, are stronger and closer than ever. This is particularly apparent as I spend my birthday watching the reunions of returning hostages with their families – a daughter collapses into her mother's embrace, young men and women jumping with exhilaration at the sight of their friend being handed over to the IDF... I see this and I see love. I see faith winning over fear. For today, at least, I will hold on tightly to this belief.

OCTOBER 7 DIARY

JULIE SZEGO

Around the one year anniversary of October 7, I speak to B'nai B'rith, a Jewish community group, on 'How October 7 Has Changed Us'.

I tell the audience that even though I had suggested this topic, I'd found myself struggling to answer my own question because to explain how October 7 has changed me I have to remember what life was like before October 7 and that's hard to do.

It is like trying to remember a faded romance or the texture of life when I was at high school.

***

7 October 2023
6.03 PM
Text from (Jewish) friend:
Another Yom Kippur war.

7.04 PM
Friend:
Omg it's so bad.

***

I tell the audience that before October 7 I never wore a Star of David necklace. And that while these days I wear a Star of David necklace, it is not to project 'Jewish pride.'

'I'm not proud to be Jewish.'

An unsettled murmur runs through the audience. After the tea break, I notice nearly half the crowd has left.

***

8 October 2023
9.12AM
Text from (non-Jewish) friend:
Israel. Fark. Love heart emoji.

9 October 2023
In the morning, I see a small group of women walking around Caulfield Park, in Melbourne's Jewish 'ghetto', draped in Israeli flags. One of the women turns her head towards the road. Her cheeks are streaked with mascara; her eyes wild with grief and horror and anger. She gathers the Israeli flag around her shoulders and marches, headlong, down the path.

In this moment, seeing my own emotions reflected in the face of this woman, I sense my life will never again be the same, and neither will I.

That evening the infamous mob gathers in front of the Sydney Opera House to burn Israeli flags, some chanting 'Where's the Jews?'

and 'Fuck the Jews'. The police arrest only a lone man carrying an Israeli flag.

The incident sets the tone for the year to come in Australia and beyond.

For some time after my mother's death ten years ago, I had an aversion to music. Listening to it felt too raw, it struck emotional chords I wasn't ready to experience. After October 7 the aversion to music returns.

The slogan arising from the Nova festival massacre is 'We Will Dance Again.'

In the weeks following the massacre, a video circulates of female IDF soldiers mock breakdancing, assault rifles slung casually across their bodies. War is on its way. But in my proxy war down-under, I do not dance. For a whole year I go without music.

Later in October 2023
First there is silence. From some friends who are no longer that. And silence from comrades and 'good' people forever emoting about this and that on social media.

Then, after the silence, barely a fortnight after the attacks, barely a week after the Israeli ground invasion of Gaza, an open letter is published in *Overland* journal, condemning 'war crimes committed by Israel in its ongoing genocide against the Palestinian people'.[1] A flood of petitions and open letters follows,[2] all of a genre: *the state of Israel is guilty since birth; it must be excommunicated from the community of nations; it is perpetrating a 'genocide'*. Never a lesser crime than the ultimate crime.

The tone is always highbrow, as in the open letter on Palestine from the 'literature and writing community', decrying '...the destruction of literature's condition of possibility in Gaza...'[3]

The petitioners don't mention hostages. They ignore or

'contextualise' October 7. They do not refer to Hamas – the very word seems taboo – let alone acknowledge that Palestinian civilians are used by them as human shields. They don't mention Hamas' chief patron, Iran. Theirs is a narrative with only one character: a malignant, murderous and treacherous Jewish state. Which all decent folks must resist by any means necessary.

The signatories are a roll call of the literary and arts world, academia, the bureaucracy, the union movement, the human rights fraternity. After a while, I'm no longer jolted by the names – prize winners, grant recipients, festival regulars who like to speak with furrowed brows about the evils of racism. They like to speak solemnly about the Holocaust.

December 2023
I resign from the journalists' union after they endorse a similar anti-Israel petition.[4] I remove myself from every group I was once part of that includes signatories to such petitions. I'm not interested in smoothing over tensions. Nor am I interested in changing one heart and mind at a time.

I'm a one-woman cancel culture regime.

I stop reading novels. The novel I was reading on October 7 remains unfinished. Instead, I re-educate myself about antisemitism, reading non-fiction books and essays late into the night, such as Dara Horn's, published in The Atlantic, one of only a handful of prestige journals prepared to run pieces interrogating anti-Zionism. Horn's piece is titled, *Why the Most Educated People in America Fall for Anti-Semitic Lies*.[5]

Late 2023/early 2024
The walls close in.

On the weekends, Melbourne's CBD is out of bounds. The

State Library puts on an exhibition of a thousand years of Hebrew manuscripts. But every weekend, anti-Israel demonstrators annex the library's forecourt. To view the ancient manuscripts, Jews must run the gauntlet of protestors calling for the dismantling of the world's only Jewish state. It is too intimidating a prospect for some, so they stay away.

Jews on an outing to the theatre, the Melbourne Symphony Orchestra or the cricket, likewise risk being hostage to anti-Israel provocations. Even our WhatsApp groups turn into unsafe spaces when our identities are leaked and disseminated to catastrophic outcomes.

We retreat into our 'ghettos' only to be targeted in our 'ghettos'. In Sydney, an anti-Israel motorbike and car convoy takes a scenic route through bayside Jewish suburbs. In Melbourne, an Islamist and hard-left mob descend on Caulfield, forcing worshippers at a local synagogue to cancel Friday night prayers. 'You don't own the streets,' thundered anonymous citizen journalist 'RonniSalt' on X at Caulfield's Jews. 'This is what fuels the hatred: this entitled sickness.'

December 2023
Stephen Fry outs himself as a Jew. He says: 'I'm frankly damned if I'll let antisemites be the ones who define me and take ownership of the word 'Jew', injecting it with their own spiteful venom. So I accept and claim the identity with pride.'

13 January 2024
Over breakfast, I read that a lesbian couple rejected a sperm donation from a Perth hairdresser because he's a pro-Israel Jew. The women reportedly said: 'We don't have the capacity to navigate parts of your identity in this donor relationship, so we are respectfully ending this now.'

11 February 2024

A writer posts on X a story about five-year-old Hind Rajab, found dead in Gaza two weeks after her family's car came under fire and she pleaded with the Red Crescent for help. The writer says: 'This is unbearable. Ceasefire now.'

I try to bear it, lingering on the little girl's photograph. She is dressed as a garden nymph with a floral halo, radiating sweetness.

March 2024

I contemplate this: the earlier, pseudo-Marxist generations of Palestinian terrorists at least made a show of denouncing antisemitism. PLO chairman Yasser Arafat famously described Jews and Arabs as 'cousins', promising the two peoples would live side-by-side in a democratic Arab-majority state once the Jewish state was destroyed.

Not so the leaders of the contemporary Palestinian 'resistance', Hamas.

Israeli journalist Ehud Yaari, a veteran analyst with sources inside Hamas, revealed some months after October 7 that on that day the ultimate ambition of Yahya Sinwar, the terror group's leader in Gaza, was to penetrate 40 kilometres inside the border to Hebron. Once there, in the West Bank, the militants would join with local cells and co-ordinate with Hezbollah in Lebanon and Iranian proxies in Syria to unleash 'an Al-Aqsa flood,' a holy war named after the mosque in Jerusalem. They might have succeeded, Yaari told The Sydney Institute, had Hamas militants not stumbled upon the Nova music festival

'There were so many girls there – good looking – and so many hostages to be taken and people to be butchered, so they stopped.'

I venture with three friends to Collingwood to support an Israeli restaurant whose owners had reportedly lost 80 percent of their trade since October 7 because... they are Israelis.

We have the outdoor courtyard to ourselves.

One friend says, choking up: 'On October 7, for the first time I imagined a world in which Israel ceased to exist.'

May 2024
A Jewish friend, a leftist, tells me he didn't really identify with Zionism or Israel. Until the 7th.

'On October 7 I realised that Israelis are Jews. And that they were killed for being Jewish.'

Later in May 2024
A Jewish friend urges me not to alienate our mutual non-Jewish friend.

'He has a great deal of affection for you,' my friend says. 'But he'll find it hard if October 7 starts to define everything about you.'

He's saying: I should try to preserve some non-Jewy parts of myself, so I don't congeal into 100 percent Jew.

And later in May 2024
After months of disruption, Sydney University invites anti-Israel campers to join a working group to review the institution's defence and security research ties for links to the Jewish state.

'This time I have words,' writes a Jewish friend after I email an article with the news. 'This reads like Germany in the 1930s. Maybe even the early '40s, with their working groups to solve the "Jewish problem".'

June 2024
On X, a regular troll calls me 'genocide Julie' and 'one of the worst Zionist propagandists in the country'. Apparently, I am on the payroll of not only the Mossad but also the CIA.

7 October 2024

We don't own the streets. We can't even own October 7.

In Melbourne and Sydney, pro-Palestine rallies are held over the anniversary weekend. In Sydney, pro-Palestine groups hold events on the 7th itself. The prime minister had urged the protest organisers to 'think about whether your cause is being advanced or set back.'

The best that can be said about Australia is that the Jew-hatred is worse in Canada and Ireland.

Later in October 2024

'I want you to understand that I don't need this thing called "Jewish",' I lecture a friend over dinner in St Kilda. I'm downing a Campari, so I'm a little flushed. 'Because it's really not worth it. Being Jewish. Not on a cost/benefit analysis. Yes, the Jewish story is rousing and beautiful, but when the price is six million dead it's not worth it.'

I go on: 'I did my bit. I even partnered with a non-Jew. Yes, I made sure my children know their history, know who they are – their grandparents were Holocaust survivors – I don't have the right not to pass on that legacy, it would be impossible not to, anyway. But I did imagine that over time, over the generations, the Jewishness of my descendants might become more diffuse and eventually disappear. And I was not as upset about that possibility as you might think. I certainly thought it was a good problem to have. Never, never could I have predicted that it would be harder for my children to be Jewish than it was for me. Not ever.'

I take another gulp of Campari.

'So I wasn't sitting around waiting for any of this to happen, you understand. I never felt less Jewish than when I went to bed on October 6.'

I recall how Stephen Fry outed himself as a Jew, claiming the identity 'with pride'.

I take ownership of the word 'Jew', because there is simply no way to divest from it. Not when non-Jews, across time and across the continents, keep failing in their capacity to 'navigate parts of my identity' as the lesbian couple who rejected the Jewish sperm donor put it.

***

At the lectern in front of the B'nai B'rith group, I say I'm not wearing my Star of David necklace out of pride but as battle-gear in what will be a long, long war.

---

1   Artists Against Apartheid, 'Stop the genocide in Gaza', *Overland*, 21 October 2023, https://overland.org.au/2023/10/stop-the-genocide-in-gaza/.

2   To cite just a few examples soon after October 7:

'Open letter from the Art Community to Cultural Organizations', *e-flux*, Notes, 19 October 2023, https://www.e-flux.com/notes/571447/open-letter-from-the-art-community-to-cultural-organizations.

Sydney Review of Books staff, 'A letter to our readers', *Sydney Review of Books*, 23 November 2023, https://sydneyreviewofbooks.com/news-and-events/a-letter-to-our-readers

UniMelb for Palestine Action Group, 'Statement of solidarity with Palestine and call to action from the University of Melbourne's staff, students, and alumni', *Overland*, 2 November 2023, https://overland.org.au/2023/11/open-letter-statement-of-solidaarity-with-palestine-and-call-to-action-from-the-university-of-melbournes-staff-students-and-alumni/.

Writers Against the War on Gaza, 'Statement of Solidarity', 26 October 2023, https://www.writersagainstthewarongaza.com.

3   'An open letter regarding Palestine from the literature and creative writing community,' *Sydney Review of Books*, 1 March 2024, https://sydneyreviewofbooks.com/news-and-events/literature-and-creative-writing-palestine-open-letter.

4   'Letter from journalists to Australian media outlets', 23 November 2023, https://www.jotform.com/form/233177455020046.

5   Dara Horn, 'Why the Most Educated People in America Fall for Antisemitic Lies', *The Atlantic*, 15 February 2024.

NORTH OF THE RIVER

SIANA EINFELD

I have lived in the north of Melbourne all my life. But, after sixteen years of loving our home in Thornbury – so close to cafés, bars, parks, our kids' local school, and with a cinema at the end of our street – in a few days, my family of four will be moving south of the river. Since October 7, from our network of a dozen local Jewish families, we are the third family to relocate. Some others will follow suit soon. Then there are those determined to stay; they refuse to be chased out of their homes by a small but virulent group of anti-Israel extremists.

Recently, I saw the peace advocate from Jerusalem, Rudy Rochman, speak in Melbourne to a full house. Rudy told us about the letters he read as a teenager written by rabbis and heads of Jewish organisations across Europe in the 1930s. The letters noted the propaganda and libels plastering their streets and in newspapers, and the escalation of physical attacks on Jews. In that correspondence the Jewish leaders reassured each other that all would be okay, that they just needed to maintain a low profile, that this uptick would soon blow over…

In Thornbury 2023, not even two days after the Hamas massacre, while we were still calling family and friends in Israel to see if they were alive, and way before Israel responded to the invasion, my suburb in the municipality of Darebin turned hostile. Our streets became covered with posters, stickers and graffiti claiming that Israel is a baby-killing regime and an apartheid state, that Zionism is terrorism, and more. On a five-minute walk to the post office with my ten-year-old son, we felt like the walls and electricity poles were screaming modern blood libels at us.

One day, as I was ripping down the offending posters on our main shopping strip, a man in his late fifties approached me to ask if I was Jewish. He pronounced 'Jewish' with such disdain that I didn't answer him. He then proceeded to say that the whole world knows that Jews are terrorists. Further down the street, another man of that generation told me not to take down the posters. When I said that the posters are spreading lies, he launched into a tirade about Israel, and when I challenged his claims, he called me disgusting and walked away. A couple of months later, I saw him in the newspaper pictured at an anti-Israel rally, next to a woman holding a placard that consigned a Star of David to a garbage bin.

On December 18 2023, Darebin City Council, which has never once passed a motion about any other foreign conflict, pushed through a motion solely condemning Israel for the war it did not start. I, too, was devastated by the humanitarian crisis and scale of human suffering unfolding in Gaza. But I also knew that a refusal to acknowledge Hamas' role in perpetuating the suffering on both sides of the border would not promote coexistence and peace in the region. The motion did not once mention the killing spree of October 7. It did not acknowledge the plight of the hostages nor the mass sexual violence perpetrated by Hamas against Israeli girls and women. We, the Jewish residents of Darebin, watched online as the group, who had attended that meeting specifically to ensure this motion passed, yelled into the council chamber, 'Shame, Israel, shame!' The motion was voted in.

As part of the motion's implementation, the Palestinian flag was raised above Preston Town Hall, indefinitely. It's the same town hall where my Israeli husband's citizenship ceremony was held more than a decade ago; his certificate was handed to him by the same councillor who brought forth the reductive motion on the Israel-Hamas war. I now actively avoid going anywhere near there.

Darebin Jews were gutted. This motion erased our pain, erased us. We also felt frightened about where the obsession with demonising Israel, and Jews by extension, was heading. We come from families who fled from Egypt, Iraq, the Soviet Union, Poland. We know all too well that expulsions start with the dissemination of dehumanising conspiracies and lies about Jews, and that violence inevitably follows.

We wrote letters and we spoke to Darebin councillors about the impact and discriminatory nature of the motion. We noted that passing it without consulting with our community – the group impacted – breached governance rules. In late December and early January, we spoke with three councillors separately. All of them admitted that they received threats, pressuring them to vote in favour, and that before and during the council meeting a group of activists kept yelling at them. We, in turn, shared our devastation at the loss of innocent life in Gaza, and our deep, deep pain over our people in Israel – grandparents, babies, children, disabled amongst them – who had just been raped, mutilated, immolated and murdered in other ways and stolen. Neither flag or both should be raised, we said, as both people are suffering, and this war should not become a competition of suffering.

We also reminded councillors that residents of Darebin include Kurds, Yazidis, Maronites and Coptics who have been persecuted by Jihadis animated by the same ideology as Hamas. We shared that my husband manages a tyre shop in Preston and that since October 7, several Iranian customers, who had lived under the oppressive Islamic Republic of Iran, gave him a hug when they learned he was from Israel.

In April 2024, our group also had an hour-long meeting with the then mayor of Darebin, a Greens representative, in the Preston Town Hall. We explained that the motion the council passed encouraged an atmosphere where anti-Israel activists were emboldened. We gave many examples, including that in February they daubed the Preston Library with swastikas. A Jewish teenager we know was so disturbed by the sight of this graffiti on his way to school that he missed a Year 12 assessment. And to get to High Street, my family had to walk past the words Glory to Hamas two-metres-high, on the back of a commercial building. We told the mayor about the deliberations that Jewish families were sharing about their future in Darebin, and about friends who avoided visiting.

The mayor appeared sympathetic. We thought she had heard us. And yet, a few weeks later, she shared a social media post of herself at the 'Darebin for Palestine' rally down High Street, where chants of 'Zionists are terrorists' and 'Resistance by any means' were recorded.

I didn't want to give up on Thornbury that easily. There was still some hope in me, so in May 2024 I joined the Darebin Interfaith Council to try and build bridges. I filled in a long application form, and was interviewed by a council representative to assess my suitability to participate. I became the sole Jewish representative, perhaps because we are such a tiny minority in Darebin. At the first meeting, I was relieved to feel welcome among about twenty members of the Sikh,

Bahai, Hindu, Catholic, Coptic, Maronite, Anglican, United Church and Muslim faiths, and to hear the suggestion of the wonderful pastor who co-chaired the council that we spend time at each other's places of worship during significant celebrations. I left the meeting with more hope that coexistence in Thornbury was possible after all. This was exactly why I had moved to Darebin in the first place, because I value and celebrate living in a multicultural community. I grew up in an interfaith family myself: my mother is Jewish, and my father is of Irish Catholic descent. During my teenage years, I loved going to my friends' faith events – confirmation, ritu kala, weddings. And I had loved having my interfaith friends at my bat mitzvah. That first meeting made me feel as if stronger social inclusion and community cohesion was within our grasp. Maybe I wouldn't need to move from Darebin after all.

My second Interfaith meeting, however, would be my last. The other co-chair, a Darebin councillor – the same one who had brought the motion against Israel in December, the same one who criticised the three councillors for meeting with 'Zionists' (meaning us, Jewish community members) – put forward a one-paragraph statement that he wanted Darebin Council to take to the Australian Council of Local Government showcase in Canberra.

Predictably, this was not a statement about housing, service delivery, disaster recovery or renewable energy. Once again it was about the Israel-Hamas war, where Israel was portrayed as the sole aggressor. I expressed my reasons for disagreeing with the statement. At that, another Interfaith member, who turned up to the meeting sporting a Palestinian flag, raised his voice at me to say that all of Israel is an illegal occupation and that yes, bad things happened on October 7, but Israel is not currently being attacked. I explained that there were thousands of rockets being launched indiscriminately at Israel from multiple fronts, that my friends and family had to run to bomb shelters sometimes several times in a day. At this point, some others in the room suggested that we shouldn't be discussing such matters at the Interfaith council when we have no impact on the conflict, and it is clearly causing more division than unity. I appreciated those sentiments, yet, ultimately, I felt alone. For me, the whole discussion had been the antithesis of what grassroots peace building should look like. Why were we not creating a community garden together, painting a mural of coexistence or cooking for people who would appreciate receiving a hot meal? I resigned from the council.

By August 2024, the little hope I had that we could remain in Thornbury evaporated. The situation for Jewish residents was only getting worse. Our friends were moving their gift shop, which had operated in Thornbury for close to a decade, following constant verbal and written threats, having their windows spray painted with racist slurs and plastered with stickers calling for the boycotting of Israel. Another friend, an Israeli, faced almost daily abuse directed at his restaurant in Darebin, including a man who yelled at his customers that they were 'supporting genocide' by eating there. And the Jewish owner of Brunswick Wine Store posted a video online where he recounted the incessant harassment he was dealing with, like a person who walked into his shop to tell him: 'We don't want your kind here.'

To get away from all this tension, my family would regularly cross town to attend synagogue on Shabbat. Once inside, we have never prayed harder for peace. Soon, however, it became clear there would be no need to continue crossing the river. We were leaving for the south anyway.

As we put our house on the market, friends kept asking me if I was sad to leave. In some ways I was. I knew I would miss our Italian neighbours on both sides, with their extraordinary vegetable patches and family passata-making days (they agree, by the way, that the Darebin council's actions were inappropriate). I would miss sourdough pastries from Akimbo Bread, and Biviano & Sons, which stocks all my favourite groceries. And being so close to some wonderful local friends, as well as my parents. But here I was, leaving. It did hurt to leave, but it hurt even more to see Jew-hatred being expressed so openly, while tolerated by so many.

As the time to go finally arrives and I pack and tape each box, I no longer feel emotional. I ask my children if they are sad about leaving the house they grew up in. Their responses make it clear that they have absorbed Thornbury's changed atmosphere more than I had suspected. My son says he does not feel sad at all. My daughter, a little more sentimental, has fond memories of playing with her friends at Pender Park, but, she says, she no longer enjoys going for walks anyway, because of the lies inscribed everywhere about her Israeli grandparents and uncles and aunts and cousins.

As the removalists take all our boxes, the fridge and the furniture, I wait for the sadness to come. When the truck drives away, I am still waiting. But I am not sad at all. I am thinking instead about the new places in Melbourne that I am heading towards. Places where, I still believe, coexistence is possible.

(UN)SAFE

KATE LEWIS

I own a finely crafted Magen David, a bat mitzvah present from my buba and zaida. I wore it on that day, then carelessly tossed it aside. It had sat lifeless in my jewellery box for over 25 years, until October 2023.

I never thought I would wear a Magen David. I saw it as a religious symbol and, while I had always felt proud of my Jewish heritage, I defined myself as a strictly cultural Jew. I loved the parts of Judaism that brought people together, the ones to do with community and family values. I felt a similar connection to Israel; it held no religious significance to me, but I loved it because it was home to the people I loved, and a community that, over time, I became a part of. My aunty Miriam, an altruistic hippy, had moved to a moshav in Eshkol, the Negev area near the Gaza Strip, in the late '70s. She fell in love with the community and, subsequently, with my uncle.

We were fortunate enough to visit my aunty, uncle and cousins often. The Australian part of our family was absorbed into the moshav community with warmth and socialist hospitality. Each visit,

I slipped seamlessly back into the idyllic lifestyle – riding quad-bikes along the deserted roads, climbing into the pool to swim at night. I drank beers, smoked *nargila* and kissed Israeli boys. I had freedom beyond anything I'd known growing up in suburban Melbourne. I felt safe in this quiet, small pocket of Israel, where no one locked their doors and, even as young kids, we were free to roam the streets until late.

While Eshkol felt like a sanctuary, somehow separate from the rest of Israel, I was always acutely aware of the tension and conflicts embedded in the country. Travelling to Israel during the Second Intifada was terrifying, in the true sense of the word. I had mild panic attacks in shopping centres, at bus stations and when walking through crowded markets in Tel Aviv and Jerusalem. Relief flooded my body only when I returned to the dusty streets of Eshkol.

On October 7, Eshkol was ravaged by unthinkable inhumanity, ripped apart and butchered. From the early hours of that morning, at the nearby Nova music festival, a massacre unfolded beyond anyone's darkest imagination, terror sweeping through the area down those streets that had once felt so safe to me. While my family sat terrified in their safe rooms, they were receiving messages on their phones that their friends on neighbouring kibbutzim and moshavim were being slaughtered, tortured and taken hostage.

My aunty Miriam's first message in our family WhatsApp group read, 'We are ok. We are in our safe room.' She listed who was with her and I realised, days later, that this might have been a kind of inventory, if one was needed. My cousin Karin was in her own safe room with her three young children, her sister-in-law Adi in another with their four kids. My cousin Paul wasn't mentioned.

'Where is Paul?' I wrote to the group as cortisol flooded my mind.

'He's in the base.'

I didn't know what that meant at the time. As soon as the first barrage of rockets was fired and the *Tzeva Adom* (red alert) was sounded, without waiting to be called up, Paul drove to the nearby Re'im army base. He found the gate unmanned and open, which was out of the ordinary. Soon after he entered, the base was swarming with Hamas terrorists. When he realised the severity of the situation, he called his nineteen-year-old son and told him: 'Take my rifle and if anyone tries to enter the house, shoot them.' Taking position on the roof of the base, Paul and two other non-combat reserve soldiers tried to drive the Hamas terrorists out. They fought them for many hours until a combat unit arrived and eventually regained control. I'm not sure how he survived that day.

Grief consumed Eshkol. Everyone lost close friends and people they loved. The kindergarten that Karin's twin boys attended was destroyed, and many of their classmates and teachers were murdered. Their best friends, another set of five-year-old twins, were burnt alive along with their brother and parents – the Siman Tov family – as they huddled in their own safe room. I thought about the Holocaust-like nightmares that had haunted my adolescence; this unimaginable reality somehow worse. I sat in disbelief as more details came through about the attacks, women raped, babies taken hostage.

Overnight, I became acutely aware of what it meant to be a Jew, and a Zionist, in the world. While grief and terror had reached new heights in Israel, tensions flared here in Australia. Jewish shops were vandalised, antisemitic signs were paraded through the city, not unlike how it was in pre-war Germany. On social media, a warped narrative gained instant momentum as the attack on Israel was labelled 'resistance' and 'freedom fighting'. Feminists who advocated loudly for women's rights all around the world fell silent about the sexual violence that had taken place in Israel. As I stood in Caulfield Park at a memorial service for the October 7 victims, I felt fear, not dissimilar to what I had experienced walking through Israel's crowded cities during the Second Intifada. As time passed, my anxiety continued to evolve. I am the granddaughter of Holocaust survivors and so this feeling of vulnerability is in my blood. Now, even dropping my children off at their Jewish school raises 'what-ifs' in my mind.

My social circle shrank. I tried to explain to non-Jewish friends why I did not feel safe anymore, but after the largest massacre of Jews since the Holocaust, at a time when I needed them most, some of my close friends disappeared. They slipped away, perhaps in avoidance, awkwardness, or maybe something darker. Before long, social invitations from my 'Northside' friends stopped coming. Against the backdrop of this war, it couldn't have been a coincidence. I no longer felt comfortable anyway, being the token Jew amongst these friends that I'd known for years. They'd felt like family throughout my twenties, when we all lived in share houses around North Fitzroy and Northcote. Now I understood viscerally the stories my grandparents had told me, about how people they thought were close friends watched on as the Nazis marched them onto death trains.

As the war kept unravelling, my safety zones diminished further. I felt vilified in almost every community except my own. I began to avoid the city and the Northside suburbs that were becoming increasingly hostile places for Jews. I no longer felt part of the progressive communities, which had once shared my inclusive values, and my respect for many in the creative industry crumbled. Artists whose work I had loved and collected turned on Jewish creatives as if we were personally to blame for the escalating war. Lists of Jews, including me, were circulated online by doxxers.

At some point, shortly after the October 7 attacks, I reached for my Magen David. I felt a weight of collective grief and trauma contained in its symbolism. I found a strange comfort touching the six sharp corners, one for each million, while recognising the irony in *choosing* to wear a yellow star.

My daughter was instantly drawn to my rediscovered Magen David, and like with most shiny things, she wanted one too. For her fifth birthday, my aunty sent her one from Israel. There was poetry in the parallel of it, my aunty Miriam, now a survivor herself, giving my daughter her first Magen David, just as my grandparents had given me mine.

My Magen David hangs around my neck now, but I wrestle with myself almost daily over the question of its visibility. It has become the physical manifestation of my inner conflict between Jewish pride and fear. Walking through the shtetl of my local neighbourhood in Ripponlea, I display it openly. It gives me the sense of belonging to something painfully significant. It's a connection to the community that I love and that I now know is incredibly vulnerable. I look for the pendants in crowds and I feel comfort whenever I see one.

The Ripponlea village has become my new sanctuary in our crumbling society. But, devastatingly, as 2024 draws to a close, the Adass synagogue at the heart of this tiny neighbourhood is firebombed. I'm not even surprised by this new low; the unchecked Jew hatred online and in the streets of Australia has literally stoked the flames. The only thing that still continues to surprise me is the silence. I received just one message of support from a friend outside the Jewish community, acknowledging the devastation after this act of terror. Is the greater tragedy that our sanctuaries are no longer safe, or that so many are silent?

HANGING ON BY A THREAD

SIDRA KRANZ MOSHINSKY

The thread arrives at my Airbnb in Jerusalem in a small cardboard box, fifteen metres long and neatly packaged. I'm going to use it as the wick in *yahrzeit* candles I'm making for the forthcoming first anniversary of October 7 – a date that looms so heavily on the horizon, it is almost immobilising.

Yahrzeit, in Judaism, marks the anniversary of a person's death; the day is set aside for remembrance and rituals, including the lighting of memorial candles. Making candles to kindle on October 7 is my small but symbolic way to honour this date. In truth, I don't know what else to do. My need to express the anguish and abandonment I have felt all year is strong, and yet, as an Australian visiting Israel, I'm an outsider. Whatever I'm feeling and experiencing pales in comparison to the realities of the people around me. Since my arrival here, I oscillate between validating and invalidating my emotions.

I'm spending six weeks in Israel, mostly to study Torah in Jerusalem but also to see my daughter, who recently moved here. In keeping with the dramatic twisting and turning of this year, the day I land at Ben Gurion Airport is the day on which Hersh Goldberg-Polin is buried. Due to the tireless efforts of Hersh's loved ones, especially his mother Rachel who emerged as a fierce advocate of the Bring Them Home movement, Hersh has become the face of the hostages. To think he and five others survived nearly a year, in conditions too hellish to fathom, only to be killed point blank by their captors just as they were about to be liberated by the Israeli army. This is yet another in a series of cruel blows. I'm staying in Baka, Hersh's neighbourhood, and stand in vigil on the side of the road as members of his family make their way to the funeral.

In looking for a meaningful way to commemorate the approaching anniversary, I suggest to my fellow scholars that we try reviving an ancient folk ritual, which I researched for a course I teach on women in Jewish history. The ritual, prominent for centuries across the Ashkenazi world, was practised in the lead-up to the High Holy Days. Led by women, it involved walking around the graves of family members. With each step, the leader would gradually release a little more of a long piece of string to create a ring, while reciting Yiddish prayers written especially for women. This string would then be cut into lengths and used as the wick of 'soul candles' lit on Yom Kippur, the Day of Atonement, to maintain a connection between the living and the dead. I wonder if performing this ancient custom, in the companionship of my peers, might help me to express some of my grief.

Would I be studying Torah and Talmud in Jerusalem if not for the events of the last year? Possibly. I had already designated this year as one in which I would create space for some of the things I had always wanted to do. Immersing myself in our foundational sources, in the land and languages from which they emerged, has long been a dream of mine. But I had not envisaged studying these holy works at a time of so much bloodshed and misery. Nor did I envisage having to take shelter as 180 ballistic missiles headed our way from Iran, part of the October 7 aftermath.

The delicate threads by which our lives hang have always been apparent to me. I'm a daughter of survivors of the Shoah, I'm a teacher of Jewish history, I've circled the sun fifty-five times. I know that, at any moment, a poor decision (mine or another's), being in the wrong place at the wrong time, the spin of the dice, can sever the connection between any of us to this world. I'm thinking of September 11, the tsunami of 2004, mega bushfires... and now this dark day. This awareness of the fragility of life can make me fearful, yet also fuels a desire to live as fully as possible in the present moment. Here I am, *hineni*.

At some point, I start noticing that threads permeate many of the texts I am studying, a motif across a range of eclectic sources. Rahab the Harlot, pivotal to the successful Israelite conquest of Jericho, hangs her crimson thread from her house as an identifier for protection. The distinguishing features of the *tallit* (prayer shawl) and *tzitzit* (tassels worn by Orthodox men) are the elaborately knotted threads attached to their corners. Legend has it that the scapegoat used on Yom Kippur to exonerate the nation's sins had a red thread tied around its horns that miraculously turned to white if the sins were forgiven. As I close the *Tanach* (Bible) at the end of each day, I place its silken bookmark at the correct page. Around my wrist is a bracelet made of red thread, a Kabbalah-inspired symbol to ward off the evil eye. In Hebrew, one of the names for thread is *tikvah*, hope. It seems as if these humble items serve as conduits of our deepest aspirations. And now I have another delicate thread in my hands that I'll soon use.

Late in the afternoon on October 6, the day wedged between Rosh Hashana and the first anniversary of the events that inverted so much of our known world, I travel with some other students to Hersh's grave to enact the ritual. His grave is situated in the largest cemetery in Jerusalem and finding it is much more challenging than I expected. *Har HaMenuchot* (Mount of the Resting) is a vast, labyrinthine city of the dead; the colour-coded sections and numbers on the graves do little to orient us. Eventually we find the one grave we are looking for amid the tens of thousands, situated at the periphery of the cemetery, with views over the hills of Jerusalem. As sunset approaches, the horizon is a little blurred, almost pastoral.

Being so recent, Hersh's grave features no formal headstone yet. It is covered with raw earth, small stones placed as remembrances and eclectic objects left by loved ones, such as handwritten notes, photographs and soccer paraphernalia. Until this moment, Hersh was a face on a poster, a graphic on a banner, a name chanted at rallies. But looking at these personal tributes, he suddenly becomes the singular person he was: a treasured buddy, a soccer team's enthusiastic fan. His death is no longer an abstraction and is what it is: an outrage; a profound, permanent loss.

Past and present converge as I stand in the loose soil next to the grave. Exactly thirty years ago, my husband and I spent a year in Israel. We might have stayed. Where would our children have been on October 7 had we done so? It's plausible they would have been at the Nova music festival, dancing, as they often do at festivals in the hills and valleys around Melbourne. But for the quirks of time and place, this could have been my child...

I take out the long wick and together, quietly, we loop it around the grave, passing the thread from hand to hand. We take turns reading out loud from the traditional texts that women used for this ritual in centuries past: 'Today we prepare candles for the sake of all these souls and for the martyrs who lie in the fields...' We cut our thread into short pieces, then find places to sit nearby where we can place the wicks on the beeswax sheets, rolling them tightly to form our candles. One of them is set aside to be given to Hersh's mother, while the others we take to light at home. I have made two: one to light the next day, another to take home to Melbourne to light on the evening of Yom Kippur.

I think of Melbourne as 'home' automatically, but as my days in Jerusalem turn to weeks, I begin to doubt where I actually belong. What does my future look like back in Melbourne where antisemitic slogans, boycotting of Jewish businesses and artists, and even violence towards Jews and Jewish sites are becoming the new normal? What if I stayed here, with its dangers, stressors and the high prices exacted?

I bring myself back. The sunset sky with its gentle blues and pinks, the solace of being in gentle communion with others, the string in my hands – these calm me somewhat. Our ritual changes nothing, but at least I have been a witness and committed myself to carrying this moment forward into my life. We wind our way out of the cemetery where a taxi driver insists on an exorbitant fee to get us back into the centre of town. I relent. Ordinary life is a blessing.

October 7 dawns. At 6:29 am I light my candle and watch it flame and melt. Can I even call this an anniversary? It's not quite a memorial day as, with many hostages still in captivity and the country at war, the events are not yet in the past. Neither is it a day of unity, given the deep divisions over the Israeli government's actions (and inactions) in relation to the hostages and the conduct of its military campaign. But it is a heavy day. I pass by cafés with black tablecloths draped over the tables; many are not even open. In parks and everywhere else I go in the city I see people sitting quietly in their heartbreak. TV stations cover the anniversary from morning till night. The sky is unseasonably overcast.

Adding to the unease, sirens go off at various times and from different places, including Gaza, targeting not only land but our sanity. There is no doubt these rockets are specially timed to inflict maximum psychological damage. I want to mourn in stillness, but instead am forced into a flurry of action. I take refuge in a shelter, a jumbled room beneath where I am staying, that smells of cat piss. I make broken small talk in English, Hebrew and French with the others gathered there – residents, visitors, a couple of workers from nearby shops.

As we huddle, I find myself pulling on my red string bracelet; nervous energy, I assume. But a kind of lifeline too. This thread is supposed to give me protection from the evil eye – in this case, the tons of airborne metal eyes angling our way. Right now, there's nothing I can do but sit here, feigning being okay for the sake of others in the crowded space. I'm not counting on this thin thread to get us through. Even so, something deep inside me reaches for it, just as I reached yesterday in the cemetery for the ritual thread.

Tomorrow, if all goes to plan, I will fly back to Melbourne. I have packed the second yahrtzeit candle, along with a little length of leftover thread. The candle will melt away but I will keep this modest thread as a tangible reminder of being at this place, at this time. I have been thrust into the paroxysms of Jewish History with a capital H. Although in reality, I was always living within its volatile narrative, just not always aware. I had naively thought I was part of the blessed generation who, born not long after the abyss of the Shoah and the zenith of achieving statehood, could inhabit a version of 'happily ever after'. But is there ever a happily ever after if you are Jewish?

These past few weeks, in what is essentially a war zone, I've experienced more physical danger than ever before. But, strangely, I've also felt uplifted as I've made my way around the streets of Israel, without the constant, low-level minority stress that has become a feature of Jewish life in Australia. I'm carrying home new learnings, perhaps a newer understanding of self. I want to work more, live more, love more, savour more. I twist at the thread around my wrist as I make my way onto the plane.

THE WINNER

LANA SCHWARCZ

```
FADE IN:
INTERIOR: ARTS CENTRE FOYER SET UP FOR AWARD
PRESENTATIONS - NIGHT

Note: The Voice Over (V/O) in this scene is
LANA's internal thoughts as she is writing her
speech. The thoughts overlay the imagined real
action.

LANA steps up onto podium. Perhaps sheds a
tear.
```

                    LANA
        Oh my god! Holy shit! Am I allowed
        to swear? Fuck it, I've done it
        now anyway. Wow! Haha. THANK you
        SO MUCH for my award!

V/O

Which I will never actually win.

LANA

I'll start by congratulating all the nominees in this category. I adore you, I adore your work and I am genuinely honoured to even be named in such incredible company. Truth be told, I'm a little surprised to win.

V/O

I won't win. I'm not an idiot. I know where I stand.

LANA

While I didn't ever dream I would need it-

V/O

I won't dream it - they won't even nominate me.

LANA

-I have prepared a speech.

V/O

I mean, which performer hasn't held their deodorant bottle as a statuette in the mirror and thanked everyone from their agent to their dog?

LANA
Now, I know it's not unusual to prepare a speech for these things-

V/O
Except if you haven't been nominated hahaha.

LANA
-but it's actually the speech I have been preparing for some time now. For everyone here who watched the Oscars, I am sure you can relate.
    (Winks.)

V/O
They don't know I am thinking of this year's Oscars of 'Jewish denouncement' and red hand pins though. Why would they?

LANA
So for my speech today, I've sculpted my words into a striking Redhead.
    (Strikes a pose, points to
      her red hair.)

V/O

Reminder to self, book hair dye appointment.

LANA

A giant matchstick so as to burn this bridge. The bridge that leads to my beautiful, imaginative, humanist, progressive, empathetic, talented community of creatives, whose hearts connect automatically with a well-written narrative or a poignant image. To some, this bridge-burning may be a shock, but after watching you over the last year,

> (Channels Jewish grandmother for levity.)

Darlinks, I do this not because I am angry, but because I am...??

> (Waits for audience to finish the sentence. They don't.)

Disappointed!
Please don't misunderstand, I am not burning you down. I don't have the will to do so, nor, despite the libel persistently applied against my people, the power. I am simply burning my connection to you, the entity otherwise known as 'the creative community of Melbourne'. My true wish for both our futures is that we continue to

move forward in peace, but
separately. A two-state solution,
if you will.

A few people start to leave.

>   **LANA** (CONT'D)
> For the last year I stayed silent.
> I was waiting to see how the final
> stages of your new 'self-portrait
> of the creative community' might
> look. I've reviewed enough works
> in progress to know not to judge
> blocks of colour that don't make
> sense yet. But I think I'm now
> getting the picture of where you
> are going with it. It's not any
> kind of picture that I would want
> on my wall.

>   **V/O**
> It's ugly, but it will sell well.

>   **LANA**
> Over the year, I watched, as you
> all parroted the same talking points
> about my people without checking
> WITH my people. Which I thought was
> weird for those whose lifework is
> creativity, which thrives on originality
> and thoughtfulness, not blanket
> repetition.

I've always believed that you – the poets, playwrights, authors, comedians – understood that words unite us in their shared definition. But then, you tossed around words in ways that dissolved their agreed upon meaning, without even opening a dictionary. And these are strong words you recontextualised, words like 'colonialism', 'apartheid' and 'genocide', words that carry enormous weight and legal definitions that should never be misappropriated. So I was surprised.

          (Beat.)

You insisted that you understood narrative. And I assumed that when it comes to knowing the mechanics of manipulating hearts and minds with the right imagery, you... were the cream... of the crop. And yet, you never interrogated the narrative you were sold; a narrative that painted my people – a minority ethnic group – as evil, thieving, powerful oppressors. How many brilliant adaptations of Yentl did we need to produce for you to understand our people better?

V/O
Don't know why I am asking that.
You boycotted it anyway.

LANA
Maybe that's the thing that hurt
most. That you'd rather check your
intel via recently falsified Wikipedia
pages[1] than with your very available
primary sources – your Jewish peers.
I mean, I assumed you were better
at exploring history, fact and
indigeneity than me, because
you are good at going to museums.
Except I was wrong. I was so wrong.
If you are indeed the expert
researchers you say you are, you
might have understood that a present-
day majority appear to be rewriting
the archaeological history of a
minority group to erase their
uninterrupted connection to an
ancestral homeland.
Thanks again for my award, by
the way.
How many of you are left here
now?
      (Shields eyes from stage
      lights. Counts remaining
      human-shaped shadows.)
Eight? Haha, well done.
      (Notices someone in the
      audience.)

Oh wow! Did you make those
earrings? I love them! Look, for
all I am saying about the creative
community, you do have really
great taste in accessories.
Especially glasses! Super fun,
always big. Anyway, I really
appreciate that eight of you have
stuck around. You're almost a
minyan.

V/O

Walk back the word 'minyan'. Explain
this is the Jewish quorum of ten
and not animated goggle-wearing
yellow beans. But too late. The
joke is lost.

A couple more exit.

LANA

Ah well.

V/O

Let's dig further into the hole.
Why not.

LANA

You know, I truly believed our
arts community's concern for
trauma triggers was real. And I
was right behind it too! Because I

agree. Art should challenge, not trigger. Then... Then you proudly paraded cool new red hands and triangles, symbols associated with historic lynchings of my tribe, on red carpets and at openings, dismissing our collective trauma. When you dug your heels in to double down, I couldn't understand your hypocrisy and why, suddenly, this trigger was 'A-OK, hunky dory and fine. Don't be so precious.' And let's be real here, you are artists, so I never mistook you for being experts at maths, but you did insist you were ahead of the pack at critical thinking. You disproved even this self-assertion, especially when it came to thinking critically about obvious numbers that don't make sense, like believing a tiny 0.2% global population of Jews controls the rest of the world. Pfff... I mean, I'm no Alan Turing, but at least I can count.

V/O
One, two, three people left....
Hey thanks for staying, Earrings!

LANA
(Bitter laugh.)
Oh, I have learned so much this last year! And I got you so wrong. Fuck it. Let's list it out.
I hear you like lists:
- I watched you target the very people who generously funded you over the decades.
- I saw you spit in the faces of Jews who founded the progressive movements that you now enjoy and have since ousted us from.
- I noted you tokenising outlier Jews without confirming if what they say is true or backed by the majority of our tribe.
- And finally, you actively compiled a list of more than 600 Jewish creatives, or you stayed silent as that list was circulated and Jews were boycotted and doxxed. And everyone, yes everyone, even you, Earrings, picked through the names and content of that private leaked chat. And with that, the picture you were painting finally revealed the totality of your overarching narcissism.
(Looks over at EARRINGS.)

                    V/O

Is she... crying? For fuck's...
Ok, be nice.

                    LANA
              (Sotto voce.)
Hey, Earrings, listen, I get it,
ok? You were just trying to do the
right thing, and you don't know
what you don't know.

Steps off podium to put arm around EARRINGS.
Sits on stage together as a pair with her.
EARRINGS is fairly bawling by now.

                LANA (CONT'D)
Shhhh... It's ok... We feel you.
But I've gotta be honest, we hurt
deeper for us. And I feel like in
the circumstances, that should be
acceptable. Don't you agree?

                    V/O
It really is a shame there is only
me, a few stragglers and the
archival videographer left to
witness this live moment. I'm
clearly biased, but as a piece of
vanity theatre, I love it. I mean,
has anyone ever won an award for
receiving an award?

Steps back on the podium.

LANA
Look, I really do thank you for my trophy. I will always, always treasure it and I'll keep it on my shelf as a reminder of something I held dear for decades. I can already hear you say, 'But if she feels that way about us, she shouldn't accept the award - it could go to someone else,' and that once again, a Jew has stolen something. But *davka*-

V/O
To be deliberately contrary-

LANA
-I'm keeping it.
    (Beat.)
I have no doubt that my speech today will be retold poorly by revisionist storytellers, and that the personal pain that I have finally shared with you will be twisted into yet another narrative that serves you. I, however, will do my best to remember you fondly, albeit with a forever broken heart.

> *Tikkun olam*, motherfuckers. See
> you on the other side. *Am Yisrael
> chai*. And Shalom.
>> (Peace sign.)

Walks off the stage. There is no one left
except for EARRINGS. Walks out the door, past
all the people who walked out and are standing
outside waiting for Lana to finish so they can
go back in for the next award presentation.
Goes home. Cries and calls Mum. Places trophy
on the shelf. Never looks at it again.
FADE OUT.

---

1   Anti-Defamation League, 'Editing for Hate: How Anti-Israel and Anti-Jewish Bias Undermines Wikipedia's Neutrality', *ADL Center for Technology and Society*, 18 March 2025.

WARRIOR OF WORDS

SHARONNE BLUM

Not long after the carnage of October 7, a well-known Australian feminist influencer declared on her platform: 'We need to expose what Jewish schools are doing and we need to undo what they are teaching'. That was the moment when the Jew-hate unleashed by the Hamas massacre catapulted me into action.

As a Jewish Studies teacher for over two decades, I have worked hard to ensure that nuance and multiple narratives are central to how we teach our students about Israel. I read the post a few times over, a quiet rage starting to build. I made my own post addressing the influencer's call to 'undo' our work. Had she spoken to me, I wrote, 'I would have told her that we teach about Israel from multiple perspectives – good, bad and ugly – [and that] connection to Israel is a central aspect of Jewishness and Jewish identity'. It wasn't my first social media post about October 7, but my targeted response marked a shift in my online presence and I started using my platform with a greater sense of urgency.

During the months that followed, anti-Jewish hostility was becoming increasingly common in my hometown of Melbourne. In one particularly shocking incident, Jewish MP Josh Burns' office was vandalised and firebombed. Distressing as it was, what impacted me most was a comment that Burns made at the press conference: that bringing this conflict to Melbourne would ultimately have no impact on the war in Israel and Gaza.

It wasn't the first time I had heard and disagreed with this sentiment, but it was a moment of realisation about the multiplicity of fronts that sets this war apart from any other conflict, expanding it far beyond an armed conflict in a faraway geographical location. It is a global war of disinformation and propaganda, often waged online, where words are distorted, weaponised and used to dehumanise Jews, particularly Israelis. It is a war of discrimination where casual racism targets Jews in a way that would never be excused for other minorities. It is a war of misrepresentation – the online space is overflowing with influencers and commentators who feel entitled to define us; to define what is, or is not, a legitimate and moral expression of Jewishness; who is or isn't a 'good Jew'. And it is a war of delegitimisation which seeks to undo the Jewish homeland and the majority of Jews who support its right to exist.

The hate spills from the online space onto the streets of Melbourne. Sidewalks, lamp posts, bus stops, footpaths, shops and walls are plastered with stickers calling Israel a terrorist state. And hateful graffiti defaces hostage posters. Our iconic laneways, a magnet for global street art fans, are no longer spaces I can lose myself in. I feel as if the walls are screaming at me – 'baby killer!' Before I enter a coffee shop, I might eye the barista and wonder if I should tuck my Magen David under my shirt. Should I roll down my sleeves to conceal the Hebrew tattoo on my forearm? And if I were to be confronted, what would I do? Would the voice I have found online serve me in real life?

As I navigate these worlds, online and offline, I feel bombarded by all the hateful words, and sometimes it feels as if I am drowning. I feel betrayed, detached from the progressive universe I once called home. Paradoxically, I am also becoming more myself every day and finding a new community of fellow warriors. This is what my life has been like this year. Feeling full and empty, angry and happy, bereft and fulfilled, connected and disconnected – I am on a perpetual emotional rollercoaster. No emotion lasts too long. This propels me to keep writing and posting. Inserting my voice into the public domain has been like a life raft, keeping me afloat.

I now write regularly for *The Times of Israel* blog, reflecting on the re-emergence of antisemitism. I have done a crash course in online content creation, making snappy and snarky Instagram posts. In one favourite, I lampooned one of these notorious feminist influencers by turning her into a red-faced hamantaschen. But mostly, my online activity offers some kind of Jewish learning, as I weave an upcoming Jewish festival or the week's *parsha* (weekly Torah portion) into the posts I create. I am still a teacher after all.

When my students come to school on Monday morning, they share stories about copping abuse on social media, on footy and soccer grounds, at nightclubs, parties and festivals. They too have been thrust into this warzone. In classrooms and the schoolyard they share their own experiences confronting antisemitism. In these moments we are students and teachers, strategists and warriors, discussing and debating the best course of action. Students help each other formulate arguments to combat online hate or suggest avenues they might take to fight the antisemitism they encounter in real life. And it is in these moments I realise that while I am teaching these young people Jewish history, Jewish text and Jewish ethics, I am also training them – arming them with the tools they need to find their voice and defend their people.

MY KITCHEN SANCTUARY

ELANA BENJAMIN

I'm standing at my kitchen counter, rolling pieces of dough into thin snakes with my fingertips, then forming them into rings to make Iraqi biscuits called *kakas*. I place each ring on a baking tray: four across, three down. Twelve per tray. I find the rolling and arranging of the dough to be soothing, meditative. I have the house to myself, sunshine streams through the window and it is blissfully quiet. But my current inner calm is a stark contrast to the world outside, which has been imploding since October 7.

Exactly a month before that deadly day, I applied for a grant to write a cookbook titled *Indian-Jewish Food: Recipes and stories from the backstreets of Bondi*. The project, I wrote in my application, would capture the delicious but little-known cuisine of India's Baghdadi Jews. This was a group of Jews who, beginning in the eighteenth century, fled Iraq for the religious freedom and trading benefits of British-ruled India. During the 1950s and 1960s, many of their descendants, my parents among them, immigrated to Australia. I felt compelled to document the food of my community before it was too late. Time was already running out: many Indian Jews who left

Bombay and Calcutta (now Mumbai and Kolkata) for Australia are no longer alive, and the rest are rapidly ageing. As my mother's 75th birthday approached, I realised I didn't know how to cook most of her traditional dishes. I wanted to learn while I still could – not just for myself, but to share with others.

In the days after October 7, I saw images I wish I'd never seen, that I cannot now unsee. I'm supposedly a writer, but I had no words for the horror and cruelty. I could not fathom that evil, that hatred. By the end of the first week after the massacre, I was overwhelmed. I knew I had to consume less news – which meant replacing my screen addiction with a different activity. I switched my phone to silent, called my mother for some recipes and headed to Coles.

I still couldn't completely disengage from the war. But now, in between reading Noa Tishby's *Israel: A simple guide to the most misunderstood country on earth* and keeping up with endless war discussions on WhatsApp, I cooked *marag* (tomato-based chicken soup) and *khichri* (lentils and rice) and boiled *chai*; I roasted potatoes and baked chocolate cake and made pizza from scratch. I knew that my pursuits in the kitchen would not bring peace to the Middle East. But these small acts of preparing food and sharing it with my loved ones lifted my spirits.

In late October, I found out my grant application was successful. I didn't realise it at the time, but my cookbook project, with the requirement that I use the grant money within a year, would similarly become my saviour in the dark months ahead.

***

Over the past year, my husband has started his day by listening to *The Times of Israel's* daily briefing. I cannot bear the onslaught of bleak news – and it's almost always bleak news – so I go into another room or ask him to wear headphones. I find the media's focus on negativity to be contagious; I absorb the bad vibes, making me feel that the world is full of hate and that I'm helpless to change it.

In contrast, when I narrow my attention to the small act of perfecting a recipe for, say, cheese *samoosas* – the cheese-filled pastries with which I've been breaking my Yom Kippur fast for as long as I can remember – it counters my despair. I've created something tangible with love, which others can enjoy and perhaps replicate. Engrossed in this activity, I can forget, at least for a while, about the dire situation in Israel and Gaza.

At the same time, I often feel guilty and wonder: shouldn't I be doing more? Nowadays, my social media feeds are filled with posts by people who seem so much more capable than me. People with families and full-time jobs who are drafting petitions objecting to biased media reporting or organising the collection of supplies and money to send to Israel, speaking up about the skyrocketing antisemitism or the barbaric treatment of women by Hamas. In contrast, my posts have mostly been about cooking, such as the photos of the *mahashas* (onions stuffed with meat and rice) I mastered under my mother's tutelage. Sure, I was proud. But also: weren't my words and images spectacularly insignificant?

Yet, with American shame researcher and author Brené Brown's words in mind – 'Stay in your own lane. Comparison kills creativity and joy'[1] – I went forward doing my best not to compare myself with anyone else (this remains an ongoing challenge), and to focus on feeling grateful for other people's strength and advocacy work.

I also reminded myself that my cookbook project was an expression of my pride in being Jewish and provided me with a deep source of sustenance. As Sam Sifton, the founding editor of *New York Times Cooking* wrote after the 2022 school shooting in Texas, 'Food is comfort of a sort, and fuel as well, for anger and sorrow alike. We cook to provide for those we love and for ourselves. In the activity itself we strive to find relief, strength, resolve."[2]

And I steadied myself knowing that I was in a position of privilege; that the grant gave me the opportunity to share something clearly Jewish and positive, and to raise awareness of a different kind of Jewish culture – Sephardi-Mizrahi – as well as to showcase the richness and diversity of Jewish community, which is often portrayed as overwhelmingly European.

Many of the dishes in my book, with their mash-up of Arabic and Hindi names, also tell the little-known story of Iraqi Jews' migration to India. (An example of this is *bamia khatta*, an okra stew that embodies two cultures; bamia is Arabic for ladies' fingers and khatta means sour in Hindi.) Fortunately, and unfortunately, the uniqueness of the Indian-Jewish experience makes it a good news story. India's Jews have the remarkable distinction of never having experienced antisemitism by Indian rulers or the Indian population. (Six people were tragically killed during the siege on the Nariman House Jewish Community Centre during the 2008 Mumbai terrorist attacks, but even that attack has been attributed to Pakistani, and not Indian, nationals.) My parents' families, together with many other Baghdadi Jews, were propelled to leave India after Indian independence in 1947 and the establishment of Israel in 1948. They left India for numerous reasons, including economic factors, Zionism and uncertainty about their future post-Raj, as they'd aligned themselves with the British, but not because they were persecuted. Interestingly, thousands of Indians are now living and working in Israel to address the shortage of agricultural workers since the outbreak of the war.

Today, fifteen months into the Israel-Hamas war, many hostages remain in captivity, thousands of Gazans have died, and there's more antisemitism than ever in Australia. So, although my cookbook is now finished and out in the world, I continue to seek sanctuary in my kitchen. This morning, inspired by the menu at Avner's – the Jewish-owned Sydney bakery vandalised with a Hamas symbol in October 2024 – I made turmeric challah dough. Turmeric is a key ingredient in Indian-Jewish food; so much so that while I was working on the cookbook, my husband coined the word *turstan* to describe the stubborn yellow stains all over our kitchen. I thought it would be fun to experiment and add turmeric to my mother's trusted challah recipe. I delighted in kneading the golden dough until it was smooth and elastic, and I'm looking forward to breaking this bread with my family on Friday night.

It's clear that in the big scheme of things, baking turmeric challah or kakas is unimportant. But in the chaotic and uncertain world we find ourselves in after the deadliest day for the Jewish people since the Holocaust, there's some comfort in knowing there's at least one area of life that's predictable and delightful.

TURMERIC CHALLAH

To make turmeric challah, add half a teaspoon of ground turmeric for every cup of flour in your usual challah recipe. If you don't have a go-to challah recipe, below is my mother Sheila Benjamin's recipe, to which I've added turmeric.

Makes two medium loaves

This recipe is a two-step process. Make the dough on a Wednesday or Thursday, then put it in the fridge until Friday, ready for braiding and baking. And if you have young children or grandchildren – or any other littlies in your life – a lovely activity is to braid challah together.

INGREDIENTS

3¼ cups bread flour (also known as baker's flour)
1 cup wholemeal bread flour*
2 tsp ground turmeric
2 tsp salt
4 tbsp sugar
7g/2¼ tsp dry yeast
1 cup lukewarm water
1 egg, at room temperature, lightly beaten
7 tbsp/140ml light olive oil

*If unavailable, substitute wholemeal plain flour or plain (white) bread flour

METHOD

1. Put the flours, salt and turmeric in a large bowl (or the bowl of an electric stand mixer) and stir to combine.

2. Put the sugar, yeast and water in a small bowl, mix well and leave for 10 minutes, or until the yeast is foamy.

3. Add the yeast mixture, egg and oil to the flour, and mix until the ingredients combine to form a dough. You can mix the ingredients by hand, or with a spoon, or with the dough hook on an electric stand mixer.

4. Knead the dough for 10–15 minutes, or until the dough is smooth and elastic. To knead by hand, tip the dough onto a floured surface. If using an electric stand mixer, use the dough hook for kneading. If the dough is too sticky, gradually add more flour.

5. Place the dough in a large, oiled bowl. Cover the bowl with plastic wrap and leave the dough to rise until doubled in size, or for 3 hours. Place the bowl in the refrigerator overnight (or for two nights).

6. At least 2 hours before you are ready to bake the *challot*, take the dough out of the fridge to allow it to come to room temperature.

7. Line a baking tray with greaseproof paper. Remove the dough from the bowl, place it on a clean surface and punch down to get rid of air bubbles. Divide the dough into two equal-sized balls.

8. Divide each ball into three equal-sized balls. Roll each ball into a long snake, approximately 30cm long, and braid. Pinch the end of the braid tightly (you may even want to seal the ends with a bit of water). Repeat so you have two braided loaves.

9. Place the loaves on the baking tray and allow them to rise for 30 minutes. Preheat the oven to 180°C.

10. Bake for 30 minutes, or until golden. Allow to cool. Enjoy!

---

1   Brené Brown, *Rising Strong: The Reckoning. The Rumble. The Revolution.*, Random House, 2015.
2   Sam Sifton, 'Grief and Cooking', *The New York Times – Cooking,* 22 May 2022.

THE WOMAN IN THE ARENA

SIMONNE WHINE

The argument exploded on a WhatsApp call. There were eight of us – members of J-United, a Jewish group I had co-founded in the days after October 7 – each with a different take on how to organise Walk for Unity, our first major event. Voices overlapped, tempers flared. We clashed over optics, strategy, and the near impossible task of balancing our fear with our urgent need to act. I listened, waiting for a pause that never came. But someone had to take charge. Leadership isn't about popularity, it's about stepping up when no one else will, even when it means being disliked. I had spent years as a project manager, honing my ability to bring order to chaos. So I took a breath and did what I do best: I asked each person to articulate their perspective, let them be heard, and then I divided the tasks and set the plan in motion.

None of us had organised an activist event before. We all had different political views and varying levels of religiosity (our group even included a rabbi) yet here we were, forced to work together as one group. Somehow, despite battles, roadblocks and countless disappointments, we got it done. And, perhaps our biggest achievement, we are still friends today.

I had never imagined myself as an activist. I wasn't part of the official Jewish leadership, nor had I ever felt the need to be. My children went to Jewish schools and that seemed like enough. Then came October 7. I was scrolling through Instagram when the images started flooding in: bloodied bodies, burnt homes, young people gunned down. This didn't feel like a war happening somewhere far away, these were my people. My blood. It could have been any of us, simply because we are Jewish. Something inside me erupted. It was as if a lion had awakened. The fear, the grief, the rage, it all merged into one undeniable feeling: I cannot stay silent.

I looked around and saw a vacuum. Our communal organisations seemed slow to respond to the swiftly rising antisemitism in Australia, caught in shock and bureaucracy. And many people felt paralysed, drowning in trauma, suffocating under a fog of helplessness. But I instinctively shifted into crisis mode, compelled to act. Taking initiative is second nature to me, an ingrained instinct built from years in leadership roles. I believe action is the antidote to fear and, in that moment, I refused to be powerless.

I began by creating Facebook and WhatsApp groups for Jewish people and allies. Just a small thing, a way to share updates and offer support. But overnight, the groups' membership grew to thousands. Strangers became a community. We were bound not just by culture and ethnicity but by something deeper, something words can't quite capture.

Walk for Unity was our response to the grief and fear that had gripped us. We set out to unite the Jewish community with our allies, to stand together not just for ourselves, but in solidarity with all cultures affected by racism. Thousands showed up at Kings Domain Melbourne. It was a clear and undeniable sign that we were not alone, and our community needed this show of support.

That event was only the start. Together with my group members, I went on to organise rallies, vigils, protests, social media campaigns, advocacy events and challah bakes to build bridges with other communities. I wanted to create spaces where Jewish people and our allies could channel their anger and grief into something productive, something that mattered.

Of course, the criticism came swiftly, and sadly it was from some of my own people.

'You're making us look too aggressive.'

'This isn't the right approach.'

'You're not doing enough.'

It hurt, but I thought back to a quote from Theodore Roosevelt's famous speech, The Man in the Arena: 'It is not the critic who counts… the credit belongs to the man who is actually in the arena, whose face is marred by dust and sweat and blood.'

Criticism had always been a trigger for me. Growing up with a deeply critical father, I was led to believe that relentless scrutiny would make me stronger. Instead, it left me bracing for judgment at every turn. But standing in the arena, I finally understood: strength isn't about avoiding criticism. It's about pushing forward despite it.

As Melbourne, the city I loved and had always felt safe in, increasingly became a place where Jews were being openly targeted, I found myself questioning everything. How could my home city, known for its diversity and tolerance, suddenly become so hostile? Each week, I watched as anti-Israel protests took over the streets. The hypocrisy was staggering. No one wants to see civilians in Gaza suffer, including me. But where was also the outrage over the brutality inflicted on October 7? The beheadings, the rapes, the kidnappings? Why was Jewish pain so easily dismissed? How could so many people react not with horror, but with justification?

To try and make some sense of it all, and as part of my increasing commitment to actively combat Jew-hatred, I buried myself in books – *Israel* by Noa Tishby, David Baddiel's *Jews Don't Count*, *Son of Hamas* by Mosab Hassan Yousef. My bedside table became a battleground of sticky notes and highlighted passages. The more I read, the more I understood that none of this was new. This had happened before. And it would keep happening unless we fought back.

I particularly cared about making Jewish voices heard. I didn't want to see our community being confined to 'Jewish suburbs', tucked away in a ghetto. Our peak bodies insisted otherwise, warning us to stay put, to be cautious. But I pushed back. I've always been a proud Jew. At three years old, I marched up to my Catholic neighbours, knocked on their door and announced: 'Hi, I'm Simonne, and I'm Jewish.' Fear was not an option. We belonged in the heart of Melbourne. We belonged *everywhere*. I insisted we stand proudly, visibly and vocally in the face of adversity. In this spirit, I mobilised hundreds of volunteers to set up an installation of red heart balloons tied to old shoes at Federation Square. This tribute to the hostages was more than a visual statement; it was a call to awareness and remembrance. Our ambassador volunteers engaged with passersby, educating them about the massacre and the ongoing plight of the hostages. The display was meant to evoke the haunting images of shoes left behind at Holocaust sites, to create a chilling link between past and present atrocities. The installation was also our refusal to let history repeat itself.

The eerie parallels to the world's inaction during the Holocaust were impossible to ignore. In another activation, we staged a protest outside the Red Cross, demanding accountability – not just for their failure to advocate for the hostages but for their historical inaction, dating back to wartime Germany. Our efforts led to a meeting between the Red Cross, Jewish Community Council of Victoria, Magen David

Adom and the Jewish MP David Southwick. While the details remain confidential, one thing was undeniable: we had started a necessary and long-overdue conversation.

Each action I organised felt somewhat liberating, like a step toward reclaiming our narrative – one that had been drowned out by a loud, hateful minority spreading misinformation. We staged another installation, this time outside Flinders Street Station, handing out yellow roses and flyers with QR codes linking to Sheryl Sandberg's *Screams Before Silence* documentary about the unspeakable sexual violence perpetrated by Hamas on October 7. To make the message even more visceral, a woman dressed in a bright yellow suit stood blindfolded and chained, symbolising the young female captives brutally abducted by Hamas. Her silent presence was haunting enough to stop many people in their tracks, prompting them to take interest in the atrocities the media refused to acknowledge.

Perhaps the most striking moment for me was when our team walked through Bourke Street Mall, megaphones in hand, reminding people that the hostages were still in captivity. Some ignored us. But many stopped. Many listened. A few even called out: 'Keep going!' Their encouragement fuelled me, making me want to do more – no matter how exhausting or overwhelming it felt at times. In those moments, I knew with absolute certainty that I couldn't stop. I *wouldn't* stop.

Even in the darkest times, there has been light. Through my activism, I have met the most extraordinary people who, in many ways, feel more like my tribe than anyone I had in my life before. Kindred spirits, driven by the same fire, unwilling to stay silent. In particular, I'm talking about my core team – Tamar and Maaian. We call ourselves The Three Musketeers. We met through tragedy, thrown together by circumstance, but what has emerged is unbreakable. We have become warriors, standing shoulder-to-shoulder, bound by a shared mission, as well as lifelong friends. Such unexpected friendships have given me strength and a deep sense of connection to the Jewish community.

One thing I have realised is that the true arena isn't a place you enter deliberately, for glory. The arena *chooses* you. I never set out to be an activist. But this war that began far away, then arrived at my doorstep, chose me. When that argument exploded on WhatsApp, voices overlapping, tempers flaring, the pause never coming, I knew I had no choice. I stepped forward, dust and sweat on my face, knowing full well that the critics would always be watching from the sidelines. But they don't matter. I will continue to fight, not just for myself, but for my children, for my people, for our future in Australia. Because history has shown us, time and time again, the cost of silence.

A DAILY UPDATE

KIM RUBENSTEIN

It was one of those indelible moments, impossible to forget, where place and time fuse and people know exactly where they were when – JFK was shot, Cyclone Tracy flattened Darwin, terrorist-controlled jetliners flew into the World Trade Centre, and more, I'm afraid.

I was with my husband and children at the ACT Jewish Memorial Centre on the evening of October 7, *Erev* Simchat Torah – an important Jewish holiday – when someone whispered to us that something terrible was happening in Israel. The details were hazy but sufficient to fill me with a deep foreboding, a sense that something core had shifted.

It was a well-anticipated Simchat Torah as, for the second time in the history of the ACT Jewish community, we had planned a separate women's reading for the following morning. We had grown the numbers of women able to *leyn*, sing from the Torah. The next morning, when we gathered to hear the leyning, we were more security conscious than usual. Without an equivalent Community

Security Group (CSG) like in Sydney and Melbourne, we just watched over the locked entrance, knowing also that today federal police would provide regular drive-bys. I noticed my own heightened anxiety as I was discomforted by the arrival of an unfamiliar woman. Rather than fully enjoying our women's service, where – unlike the Orthodox tradition – every woman attending the ceremony was called to the Torah, I'd occasionally glance over at the newcomer with apprehension (I pray that it was not discernible).

The community's security has been tightened since that day. Our building is in walking distance of Parliament House, Canberra, with its distinctive flagpole clearly visible as we look out the window during synagogue services. In 2025, following the firebombing attacks on synagogues in Melbourne and Sydney, we now have a permanent security guard, in addition to professional guards during services and events.

These are welcome and unwelcome changes to our community. Unfortunately, vigilance can be uninviting, while openness can be too inviting. It is always a question of balance, a word which has become even more important since October 7.

My personal sense of balance and equilibrium was altered as I became intensely concerned for family, friends and colleagues living in Israel. It was hard not to think about them all the time, but I knew it was important to maintain my mental health and to be meaningfully connected to what was happening around me. So, I established some routines, and for a significant period after October 7, I'd start the day by checking the news about Israel and Gaza, before moving to focus on my own life in Australia. In this way, the conflict would not overshadow my entire day.

One of the first things I'd do on waking up was to open my WhatsApp to read an anticipated message from one of my colleagues in Israel, Dr Yofi Tirosh.[1] I had met Yofi five years earlier, when I was a visiting professor at Tel Aviv University Law School, and we remained connected through our common research interests, such as gender and public law, and our aligned commitment to public policy. I had reached out to her just after the Hamas massacre and she wrote back:

> *Dear friends, thank you for your caring and concerned messages. I am unable to answer them individually. Sharing a short update after a very long second day of this inconceivable war. The situation is beyond words. Simply horrific. So many people we know, former students, neighbours from my childhood are either dead, wounded, captive in Gaza, or simply absent and there is no contact with them. The numbers keep rising. As you know, the reality in Israel is always very complex, moving from one emergency to the next, but I simply do not have categories available to me, a vocabulary, for making sense of the events.*

And yet Yofi found a vocabulary, and a fine one at that, providing us daily updates of her experiences. She wrote about her partner volunteering in a cucumber field. She described a joint Shabbat dinner in her building in Tel Aviv where each neighbour shared a practice that gave them some comfort or relief, a dinner shortened by the air-raid sirens and booms of missile interceptions a few kilometres south which sent them to their shelters. She told us how she tried a fly-fit yoga class where you hang, stretch and role on long, elastic, colourful hammocks from the ceiling and her 'wondering whether it was appropriate to describe to you the joy of body and playfulness, and to pause on a normal and positive moment amidst the pain'. She followed this by a post quoting her yoga teacher telling the class: 'Some people feel uncomfortable closing their eyes these days. That is OK, you may keep them open.'

Yofi's daily messages anchored me, giving hope by reminding me of the community spirit and volunteerism in Israel, and the fact that people there were still able to find some joy in their daily lives.

I, in turn, kept Yofi in the loop of things happening in Australia, of how my life had been altered here. In December 2023, for example, I wrote to her:

> *One of my many 'to dos' today is to draft a letter of resignation, which will be used to guide others in a similar position, to resign from my union – with a heavy heart. I became a member of the National Tertiary Education Union in February 1993 and for 30 years have been a believer in workers' rights and the importance of collective action. But after trying to get the central leadership to openly distance itself from disturbing and alienating statements made by many union branches (in the union's name) that fail to acknowledge October 7 and fail to acknowledge, let alone call for the release of hostages, the time has come. And I should say I'll be joined by many non-Jewish colleagues too – so disheartened by the tribalism and lack of nuance. The alienating statements have made many members feel vulnerable in their own workplaces.*

Yofi wished me 'emotional strength' as I moved forward. In her next missive to us collectively, she said:

> *Yesterday I complained. I am asking myself what is the emotion associated with that complaint? I think the most dominant emotion is fatigue.*

No wonder then, that soon after Yofi sent us what she wrote would be her last daily update:

100 days since October 7. I wish we could bracket this time meaningfully. I wish it was not just a round and thus, a symbolic number, but an actual milestone for something. But it isn't. There is no closure or turn of events. There is currently no sign of relief or change underway. It is yet another day of immense pain, anger and uncertainty. For this last daily message, I tried to make a list, an intermediate summary, an inventory of where we are with the hostages, the displaced, the fighting in the south, in the north, in the occupied territories and in the Red Sea, and the global aspects of all this. I gave up on this endeavour pretty quickly. It was paralysing. I have been an activist all my life. Activists are, by definition, hopeful. I am tired. Very tired. And deeply worried. I am struggling to find reasons for hope and sources of energy. Writing these daily updates has been anchoring for me. It was a way to approach this hard-to-fathom reality incrementally, adding one small piece after another to the tapestry. The magnitude of this war, its many dimensions, the multiplicity of death, of violence, of horror – it is probably impossible to make sense of it other than through the concrete. Thank you for being there. Thank you for caring. For now, I am pausing. With gratitude to you, and with dreams and wishes for peace. Shalom from Tel Aviv.

I am still in touch with Yofi, but relationships with colleagues closer to home have also sustained and grounded me in these last fifteen months. A message from one of my non-Jewish Australian peers was particularly meaningful: remember to 'spare some time to do something nice every day that reminds you of what the world could be – the just and feminist world we're working towards, despite these dark times.'

I am finalising this piece, just over a year after Yofi's last daily update, with a measure of cautious but profound relief, as today marks the commencement of the first stage of the 2025 ceasefire agreement. I passionately hope that this significant development enables a path towards meaningful change. We all have a role to play in continuing to work towards social cohesion at home and an enduring peace overseas, towards the kind of world where, as per Isaiah's prophecy, 'Nation shall not lift up sword against nation, neither shall they learn war anymore.'

---

1   Lihi Ben Shitrit, *The Gates of Gaza: Critical Voices from Israel on October 7 and the War with Hamas*, De Gruyter, 2024.

THE WOMEN'S CIRCLE

SHARON SZTAR

We gathered in circle under a clear sky in the Byron Bay hinterland. Our chosen meeting place, an outdoor temple rotunda set against the majestic Mount Jerusalem. It was there that we wept and prayed, paying homage to our murdered and captive sisters. As the sun made its way to the horizon, we lit Shabbat candles – a symbol of our trust in the light, even in the darkest of days – just like the women of our kin have done for over 4000 years. One of us began to sing the uplifting psalm *Shir Hamaalot* to close the ceremony, and when our twenty voices joined her, something primal awakened in me.

In the preceding six months, I'd felt rattled and isolated. I'd been filtering my words at local Northern Rivers women's get-togethers, because I no longer felt safe to speak freely and openly. The global silence about what happened to the women of my tribe on October 7 had permeated these spaces that I had belonged to for more than a decade. Whenever I had tried to challenge it, I was met with disinterest and, in some cases, explicit disregard. Where were the strong feminist voices? Why weren't they demanding our girls be released from captivity? Where was the outrage about the desecrated bodies of the Nova festival's young partygoers?

I invited the women in our local Jewish and Israeli network to come together on International Women's Day 2024, to honour our mixed feelings about the day and the movement that no longer seemed to represent us. Huddled together in that beautiful hinterland setting, a vital conversation about what it means to be a Jewish woman at this juncture in history unfolded. I felt a grounding and belonging I'd not sensed for a long time. It had been so easy, so very easy, to create this safe haven because, even before we met, we were bound by a bloodline.

To continue nurturing our sisterhood, several of us committed to holding regular gatherings, aligned with the Hebrew lunisolar calendar. Given my significant experience running women's lifecycle circles, I offered to facilitate the sessions. Our early events were small and intimate, but as word spread the group grew to more than forty members – aged eighteen to eighty – from within and beyond the Northern Rivers borders.

These monthly circles have helped me navigate the hurdles of life post-October 7 and provided much solace. I have had nowhere else to take my rising angst, resulting from what has felt like a barrage of bullets, as I go about the routine of daily life. It isn't just women's groups where I have felt like an outlier since the war began. A simple walk down the street, an overheard conversation at a cafe, my social media or Substack feed – everywhere I turn, old allies with whom I used to share confidences and sit in peace-loving workshops, now speak with contemptuous zest against Israel and Zionists. Shortly after October 7, at a local *kirtan* (chanting festival), half the audience chose to stop dancing when the musicians sang in Hebrew.

One of the bullets that struck most deeply was the 2024 Byron Writers Festival. This time I turned up as a cautious observer, rather than the keen participant of previous years. Before I even arrived, I felt unwelcome, knowing that no Israeli or Jewish voices were being represented in the scheduled sessions about the Middle East conflict. Rather, John Lyons, a non-Jewish Australian foreign affairs journalist, took the stage several times as the lone expert. Well-known for being critical of Israel, he was invited to discuss his book *Balcony Over Jerusalem*, which had been published seven years earlier. When he received a standing ovation, I was crushed to see people I knew clapping and cheering. Then, there were sessions where the history of Indigenous Australians was conflated with that of the Palestinians, while the speakers ignored Jewish indigeneity to the land of Israel, and the audience was encouraged to chant *From the River to the Sea, Palestine will be Free* alongside the Acknowledgement of Country. At that festival, my feelings of being ostracised from a community of fellow creatives and artists – those I once believed were the truth seekers of society – were cemented.

Ironically, one of the reasons I moved to the Northern Rivers twelve years ago was because I assumed – as many of us freedom seekers, nature lovers, refugees of the busy modern world did – that this community was all-inclusive. Up until October 7, I had never specifically sought the company of Jewish people. On the contrary, I lived what one could call an assimilated life. My circle of friends included Aussies, Greeks, Italians, Poms, Germans. It didn't matter, did it? We are all human beings, aren't we?

But had I only been accepted into diverse groups in the past because I blended into the crowd, straightening my dark curls so that those who knew me could forget who I really was? And did I camouflage so well that I sometimes 'forgot' to tell new people I met that I was Jewish? I have asked myself these questions time and again this past year. Did I do it wrong?

Some time ago, I heard an Aboriginal elder speak about self-preservation. She told the audience how after challenging events, her community would often retreat into their own Mobs to nourish, recover and rebuild before facing the wider public again. Perhaps that was what our Jewish women's circle was becoming too – our place of sustenance. A place where we could tend to our roots to grow healthy branches.

To honour our connection to the land and lore of Israel, we have tracked the motifs of the Jewish calendar months from the darkness of *Av* to the trust and faith of *Elul*, to the birthing of a new year in *Tishrei*. We have remembered our foremother Rachel and the mother energy of *Cheshvan*, and have spoken to the powerful attributes of Miriam the Prophetess in the month of *Nissan*. We built a wailing wall with large stones from a local river, danced to the divine, planted seedlings in pots. We open and close each circle gathering with a psalm or traditional song. Singing in Hebrew has been an essential element of our healing. I've noticed it's irrelevant if my mind doesn't understand all the words, because my body still feels the beat and my heart recognises the melody. Through this circle, we tap into something ancient, mysterious and comforting.

Half-way through the year, we began to reconnect with the non-Jewish community. As part of a broader Northern Rivers Jewish community event, I designed a panel discussion, Healing the Sister Wound, with the intention of building a bridge with the wider sisterhood by sharing our history, customs and current emotional landscape. My fellow speakers and I told the story of our four Jewish Matriarchs and discussed what it was like growing up in both Israel and the diaspora. When we opened the floor to the audience of more than a hundred people, one non-Jewish woman cried: 'I'm sorry!' Tears fell, hugs were extended, hands were offered. I left feeling lighter – seen and heard.

As often happens with circles, the ripple effect has generated more of them. Soon, one of the non-Jewish attendees reached out with a request to expand our outreach initiative to some of her female friends. On a warm spring Friday night and new moon, eleven of us gathered in her home to conduct a Sister Shabbat ceremony followed by dinner. We were nervous at the start, as we'd never shared our spiritual rituals in such an intimate manner with those outside of our cultural circles. But our hostess and her friends engaged generously and deeply with our candle-lighting, wine and challah ceremony as part of welcoming the Shabbat Queen. For the first time since October 7, I felt at ease again in a diverse women's group.

That initial circle on International Women's Day, and all that has grown from it, has given me the confidence to walk differently in the world, and specifically in the Northern Rivers, as a Jewish woman. I'm no longer a camouflaged Jew; I'm all of me, intact and on display. Even though the anti-Israel and anti-Jewish sentiments still live on in the region, my newly embraced acceptance of who I am, together with the blossoming of new friendships and collaborations, has provided me with a strong and solid backbone. I appreciate that my tenacity – and our tenacity as a people – comes from knowing we may fall, but so too do we rise. Over and over – just like the moon we gather around each month.

AND STILL WE DANCE

RABBI JACQUELINE NINIO

Simchat Torah. A holiday which marks the completion of the annual cycle of reading the Torah in synagogue. It is a time of celebration: singing, dancing in circles, people whirling with abandon while holding the sacred Torah scrolls. But in October 2023, as the band played and the congregation, where I am a rabbi, rejoiced, I sat alone in my adjacent office. I could not participate in the festival because, less than two weeks earlier, my father had passed away after a long illness.

Since the day he took his last breath, I had not stopped. I wrote the eulogy, prepared the funeral service and sat with my family in our grief. Because Dad died the day before Yom Kippur, the Day of Atonement, one of the most significant Jewish holidays, the usual seven days of *shiva* (ritual mourning) had been cut to just a few hours. (When someone passes away during the High Holiday season, the traditional grieving timeline is sometimes reduced). I received an outpouring of messages and expressions of care from my friends and community. But before I knew it, I had stepped back into the hectic pace of rabbinic life – officiating at a wedding, leading services and preparing the upcoming Sukkot celebrations.

In my office on that fateful day, I was grateful for the opportunity to retreat – to listen to the music from across the courtyard – knowing the congregation understood why I could not be there. I remember sitting there, wondering how I would navigate the challenges of the year ahead whilst dealing with my loss.

Slowly, murmurs filtered into the cocoon of my mourning. Something was happening in Israel, but at that point, none of us understood the magnitude of what was unfolding. None of us anticipated the path of shared grief that lay ahead of us all.

***

Following the death of a parent, Jewish people recite the *Kaddish*, a prayer giving thanks for the gift of life, every day for eleven months. This prayer must be said in the presence of a *minyan*, at least ten other adults. Every morning, surrounded by members of my congregation, I recited the ancient words that contained my grief, the music of the Aramaic connecting me with the past while I contemplated my present loss, remembering my dad.

It was the same for our community after October 7. We found comfort and strength in gathering together to recite the familiar melodies of prayers, our voices raised as one. Almost everyone had a connection to someone who was murdered, kidnapped or injured that day in Israel. We all had family and friends who were being called up to defend Israel, now vulnerable in a way we had not imagined possible. The old words took on a new resonance: prayers about releasing hostages, passages we thought had been relegated to history, felt to us palpable; we could sense our ancestors' pain. And we recited the names of the hostages and their families, whom we would come to know intimately. They became a part of our rituals. Every Shabbat service we added new prayers, a candle for the hostages, another for all the lives lost in the conflict. Touchstones, to acknowledge the pain.

Just as the recitation of Kaddish gave me a daily space to acknowledge my feelings, our synagogue services offered our members a space to express their emotions – grief, anger, fear, vulnerability. For many, the wounds and trauma of the past had been reopened. This was the case for me too. My father and his family had been forced to leave their home in Egypt due to antisemitism in 1956. And now anti-Jewish hate was on the rise again, across the world and on our own shores in Australia. In the face of it all, I tried to make our synagogue a haven, a space to have difficult conversations and sometimes just to hold each other.

Some congregants sought me out to ask if, in the wake of the atrocities, it is appropriate to have a bar mitzvah party or a wedding celebration. Just as I sat apart at Simchat Torah, unable to dance, the community was asking: should we dance? As we have done so many times during this crisis, we looked to our ancestors. After the destruction of the Temple, people wanted to stop living. They asked the same questions. The rabbis of the time said: not only can we find joy, we *must* find joy. Our joy is our act of defiance.

And so, on Simchat Torah, the one-year anniversary of October 7, we gathered and we danced. My year of mourning had ended and I was able to join the circle. There was a heightened sense that we danced not just for ourselves, but for our people, for our very existence. Instead of the seven joyful *hakafot* (ritual circuits), however, we stopped halfway and did one silent circuit around the central platform to honour the hostages, the ongoing deaths and the antisemitic acts in our own country. It was a haunting moment to acknowledge our pain. Then the music surged, and we returned to celebrating with even more fervour than before.

***

My year of mourning came to an end, but there has been no such closure for our community. Since the anniversary of October 7, antisemitic violence has only escalated. In our neighbourhoods, hateful graffiti has been painted on homes, cars have been torched, a synagogue and a childcare centre set on fire. Our children's schools are more guarded than ever. We have been supported by many non-Jewish people who send messages of comfort, who reach out to say 'this is not Australia', 'this is not who we are'. But we are still feeling vulnerable and afraid, and there is a sense of disbelief that this is happening in Australia, the haven so many of our families fled to and embraced.

Our challenge now is to hold on to hope. Throughout thousands of years of history, no matter what has befallen us, Jews have defiantly continued to pray and dream of peace. It takes great courage to believe that there will be a better tomorrow, that we will dance again in freedom.

JEWISH ENOUGH

NOÈ HARSEL

We all huddled together in the cold. The fog hung heavily over the field, like a secret. Our breath made disappearing soft clouds as we pulled scarves tighter around our necks and watched our boys kick a soccer ball. The white numbers on their jerseys hovered in the mist. The conversation turned, as always, to October 7. Some parents said their kids covered their Jewish school uniforms on the way to and from school, hiding signs of their identity out of fear. Mine didn't wear such uniforms – they attended public schools – but they weren't untouched by the rising tide of antisemitism. The other mothers shook their heads. Their eyes landed on me. I took in my breath, used to this feeling. Someone wanted to say something that I wasn't sure I wanted to hear.

'At least you're lucky,' one woman said. She squeezed my arm and gave me a smile. 'This wouldn't be affecting you so much. You know, not being… you know, not really Jewish.'

It would be great to pretend that I had a clever response ready. Instead, I just stood there, mouth open. She had known me for decades.

***

I grew up in what can be described as an American-Jewish, culturally liberal, left-leaning community, and with many school friends who were like me: mixed-race and from mixed cultures. And in this privileged environment, having a Japanese mother and a Jewish father, whose family escaped the pogroms in Tsarist Russia, it didn't warrant much conversation. I was simply me – an Asian Jew. At home, we celebrated the High Holidays and went to Congregation Beth Shalom. My Jewishness then felt solid, not a battleground to defend or a riddle to solve. It was just who I was.

Coming to Australia as a pre-teen in the '80s, finding a place in Melbourne's Jewish community was not straightforward for me. My parents – reserved and, quite possibly, snobs – didn't seek out the community and we definitely didn't fit into its tight-knit circles. At the time, I felt like an outsider, unmoored from the rituals and rhythms that everyone else seemed to understand without thinking. But as I got older and found my way into work as a writer, producer and curator, I formed friendships with a group of Jewish creatives. They weren't religious, not in the sense of attending shul or following any particular observance. Their Jewishness was cultural and expansive, stitched together in ways that mirrored my own. They didn't raise eyebrows at my lack of a Jewish school education. They put up with my blessings during Jewish rituals we celebrated together, said in a muddled mix of Japlish, Yiddish and Hebrew – the way I had heard them growing up. They ate my High Holiday meals, cooked with miso and soy. They let me in, made space for my awkwardness and, in their way, showed me I could belong – not perfectly, but enough.

So when, eighteen months ago, I stepped into the role of director and CEO at the Jewish Museum of Australia, it wasn't something that I stumbled into by accident. I wanted to fully enter into the community whose door, I had always felt, was only half-open for me. I did suspect that being an Asian Jew and leading a major Jewish organisation could mean that some people would have questions about my background. But I hoped that it would just be a momentary curiosity, that soon enough we'd all turn our attention to the real work. I believed that once I proved myself, the noise would fade. I thought it would be that simple.

Then, three months later, came October 7. The questions about my Jewish identity – raised both within and beyond the Jewish community – were quickly overshadowed by what came next.

Social media feeds became awash with, at best, casual indifference to the increasing antisemitism, and at worst, outright Jew-hatred. Writers I had privately collaborated with, artists I had admired and knew, heads of organisations I had supported and worked with – some of whom had sat at my Shabbat table – expressed views about Israel and the war against Hamas that framed Israel as the sole aggressor, dismissing any complexity or shared culpability.

As a Jewish person, I've always understood that the world rarely fits into neat and simple categories. Ours is a culture of passionate debating. In any Jewish conversation, you can guarantee multiple versions of a story and an endless array of perspectives. I was taught to question everything, and when I feel certain, to question again – especially then. I had always believed the arts sector shared these principles, embracing complexity and resisting absolutes. But after October 7 I saw I was wrong. It was disorienting. Were these not some of our brightest minds – those we rely on to grapple with nuance and question assumptions? Instead, came the brash and unequivocal declarations that Jewish people control all the money and hold all the power, that Jewish artists shouldn't get awards, that Jewish shows should be cancelled and Jewish businesses not patronised.

One of my oldest friends, who isn't Jewish and is a writer, told me she didn't understand why her social media posts were affecting me so deeply. Naively, I tried to explain. I told her how it felt to see her sharing posts from prominent Australians mocking Jews as hysterical and irrational in the wake of October 7. I tried to convey how deeply those words cut, how they weighed on Jewish hearts already burdened with grief and fear. She listened, then brushed it aside casually and cuttingly with: 'Well, I never saw you as Jewish.'

It wasn't long after this that the questions about my identity reemerged – questions that often felt less like curiosity and more like accusations. Was I Jewish enough to lead a Jewish museum? Was I Jewish enough at all? The questions didn't just come from outside, they also echoed in my mind. My Asianness, too, often came under scrutiny. You don't look Japanese, people would say, as if identity could be distilled into a single, visible trait. I lived in a constant state of uncertainty. Where did I fit in, and who, if anyone, had the right to decide?

***

If my Jewishness was under scrutiny in some spaces, in others it became a label thrust upon me whether I liked it or not. I found myself in a professional setting where I expected solidarity, only to be met with silence, hesitation or even resistance, when I raised concerns about anti-Jewish sentiment. The focus would shift, slipping away from the prejudice itself and onto me – my identity, my affiliations, whether my concerns were even valid.

When I finally used the word 'antisemitism' to describe the growing bigotry I was witnessing at the organisation where I was a board member, the response was not acknowledgement, but avoidance. Instead, some people with vested interests proceeded to explain antisemitism to me, of all people, as though it wasn't a prejudice I understood first-hand, a prejudice that affected me. 'There have been concerns raised about having a Zionist on the board,' I was told. The words, delivered with careful neutrality, landed like a slap. Was my Jewishness now a problem?

At the same time, I was hearing from artists in our museum who were frightened – afraid of being known as Jewish artists, worried that their identity alone might put their careers at risk. I saw their work disappear from programs, their names quietly dropped from projects, their presence erased online. Meanwhile, people from both Jewish and non-Jewish organisations began reaching out, asking for advice, for support – unsure of how to handle the unease that Jewish identity now seemed to provoke. There was a growing sense of isolation, of being simultaneously hyper-visible and invisible.

***

A close friend recently told me that after October 7 she'd started to see me as more Jewish than she ever had before. This is not something that I am yet ready to claim as a victory. I am not sure what it means to be 'Jewish enough'. I am not even sure that I need to figure it out. I have spent most of my life on the edge of enough – not white enough, not Asian enough, not Jewish enough. Over the past fifteen months, the world has felt sharper, harsher. Certainty is everywhere. People rush to declare their 'truths' as if they have found the only answers. I don't have this urgency. I don't need to cling to absolutes. I continue living on the edge – a place where everything is fluid, where the answers only lead to more questions.

As the Jewish Museum faces relentless waves of online hate, I have stopped worrying about how people see me. I have found my footing through action. My team and I work to create light for the Jewish community by providing safe spaces that celebrate our culture – stories of our shared histories, songs of resilience and images of hope. We also invite other Australians to share in the spectrum of all these moments. My hope is that everyone there can feel 'enough'. And maybe this is the most Jewish thing I've ever done.

A MESSAGE FROM MY FRIEND

JESSICA BOWKER

A few months ago, I woke up to a six-minute voice message from my non-Jewish friend and the godfather of my youngest son, based in Los Angeles. It began: *Dear Jessica Bowker, this is my verbal letter to you. I just wonder if I'm about to step over a line, but I'm pretty sure our friendship can take it…*

My pulse quickened as I wondered what lay beneath this ominous preamble. But as my friend continued and I absorbed his words, the tension in my body dissipated. His message was in response to recent posts I'd shared on social media about antisemitic incidents in Australia. I posted a photo of the words *Gas the Fucking Jews* scrawled on a pole in Melbourne, then a news story about students from a Sydney Catholic high school performing Hitler salutes and targeting Jewish students.

The gist of my friend's message was: if you look for examples of hatred, you'll find them, it will drain your energy, and you'll amplify hate at a time when more love is needed.

This message prompted me to flip the script and reflect on the unexpected silver linings that have emerged because of October 7, particularly how my friendship circle has expanded and become stronger.

One of the first people who reached out to me after October 7 was also the only Palestinian person I know, the mother of a boy at my son's school. The previous year, she'd returned to Perth after living in the Middle East with her family, and we got to know each other when our sons became friendly. We gravitated to each other, probably because of some similarities between us and out of mutual curiosity. We both grew up in tight-knit families and moved across countries, and we now live in multicultural Perth. Our families are of mixed faith; mine includes Jews and Christians and hers, Muslims and Christians. We both avoid pork, but otherwise we lead secular lives.

Feeling disillusioned and forever changed by October 7 and the war in Gaza, we've become much closer. While many of our Perth friends are unaffected by this conflict, for us it feels painfully close to home. We've been in turmoil for more than a year, unable to distance ourselves from this ongoing tragedy, and we realised early on that we had much in common and needed each other.

This became clear when, shortly after the war began, we went for a walk around the lake and my friend asked: 'Are you a Zionist?' I was prepared for this, but not for the question that followed in her next breath: 'And can you explain what your understanding of Zionism is?' I felt a rush of relief to hear the openness in her question, and even though I suspected she might find my response unsettling, her desire to understand was sincere. Such mutual curiosity has become the bedrock of our friendship, allowing us to navigate difficult topics and learn from each other.

I told my friend that Zionism is the belief that Jewish people have the right to self-determination in their ancestral homeland and that Israel has a right to exist. That, as a Zionist, I acknowledge both Israelis and Palestinians are deeply connected to the Holy Land, and I believe in peaceful co-existence between them. Surprised by my explanation, my friend said she hadn't heard Zionism described this way before.

That day by the lake, I also shared with my friend how I felt coming to her home the first time after our boys met. She had family visiting and my son had stayed over for dinner. The warm atmosphere there reminded me of our family gathering around my grandmother's Shabbat table, with laughter and animated conversation wafting through her home. And my friend said that even before she knew I was Jewish, she felt there was something familiar about me: 'You looked just like one of us!' We joked that we probably share DNA somewhere along the line.

During one of our long phone calls, I asked my friend if she has conversations like ours with anyone else. Because she's my first Palestinian friend and I'm her first Jewish friend, there's a unique quality and a growing depth to our relationship. We talk freely; nothing is off limits. As we discussed the complicated history of the Middle East conflict, she told me her father's family were forced to leave their home in 1948; they've never been able to return. And I explained how many of today's Israeli Jews had lived as second-class citizens in the surrounding Arab countries, before being forcefully expelled and never allowed to return to their homes either. Acknowledging the agony of both peoples, we agreed they must find a way to live together.

We also veer into the difficult territory of discussing the October 7 atrocities, the Israeli hostages, and the devastating war in Gaza. We talk about life for Palestinians under occupation and for Israelis under constant threat from the Iranian Revolutionary Guard via its proxies Hamas, Hezbollah and the Houthis; and about the global explosion

Jew-hatred accelerated by the war. Sometimes, we compare our [so]cial media feeds and are shocked by how different they are. We [se]e how misinformation is being weaponised to drive people further [a]part and we talk about how cautious and discerning we have to be.

These conversations require patience and energy, but we persevere, always hearing each other out. As we stood talking in a carpark the other day, I broke down expressing how grateful I am that we've reached this point where we can be open with each other. 'It's not easy at times but I'm glad we haven't given up on each other, this is worth it,' I said, embracing my friend. And she replied, 'Me too, I'm so glad you said that.'

I've also linked up with two other people connected to the Middle East – one in Perth and the other in Jerusalem – who were strangers to me and each other before October 7. Today the three of us are regularly in touch.

Soon after the Israel-Hamas war began, I reached out to Perth author Tess Woods after seeing her social media post that expressed compassion for both Israelis and Palestinians. I was drawn to Tess because she demonstrated a more measured and nuanced understanding of the conflict than many others in the arts community who espoused lopsided anti-Zionist rhetoric, and she was open to hearing different perspectives. At the time, I was feeling despondent and alone as a Jewish writer in Perth.

Tess responded immediately and we bonded over our connection to Israel and Palestine through my Jewish and her Christian Arab heritage. I felt safe opening up to Tess because she was so unguarded with me. During one of our lengthy late-night message exchanges, I told Tess that I'd stopped wearing my Star of David necklace in public after the antisemitic protests at the Sydney Opera House. That my heart sinks every time Jewish creatives are cancelled or made unwelcome in cultural spaces. That I did not attend the Perth Writers Festival, fearing antisemitism might rear its head there too. Thankfully, with people like Tess involved in the event, the festival went ahead without any issues.

Around the time I connected with Tess, I stumbled upon a podcast co-hosted by Jerusalem-based Australian-Israeli peace educator, Ittay Flescher. In the wake of October 7, I had developed an unhealthy attachment to my phone, spending hours online trying to make sense of the war and the history of the conflict. Ittay presented one of the most enlightening perspectives I'd heard on the topic, exposing me to Israeli and Palestinian voices I hadn't heard before and platforming people who are committed to peace building and a shared future in the Holy Land.

I messaged Ittay to thank him for creating the podcast. Once he responded, I asked him more questions and we began exchanging more messages. Around that time, my thirteen-year-old son was targeted at school for being Jewish. Grappling with how to tackle this, I asked Ittay, a former high school teacher, for guidance, and he directed me to educational resources and offered his support from afar.

When I shared Ittay's podcast with Tess and my Palestinian friend, they were equally moved by it. My Palestinian friend is now also in touch with Ittay, and she was excited to tell me about their recent video call, where he gave her a walking tour of Jerusalem.

Tess is regularly in touch with Ittay too. A few months after they connected, Ittay told Tess that he'd written a manuscript describing his vision and hope for the shared future of Israelis and Palestinians. Tess was bowled over. She sent the manuscript to her Australian publisher, who then took on *The Holy and the Broken*. It was a joyful, full circle moment when Ittay called from Jerusalem to tell me that his message of tolerance would soon reach a global audience at a time when such messages are desperately needed.

My connection with Ittay has also produced another unexpected silver lining. Despite attempts to educate the students at my son's school, over the last year he has continued to be repeatedly bullied for being Jewish. Among all else, he has had students shout at him 'Hitler was great!' and 'Fuck the Jews!' One student refused to sit next to him on the school bus because he supports Israel. After the twelfth (!) antisemitic incident, my husband and I met with the school to discuss how to address this issue with sensitivity, in a way that can bring people together and build bridges rather than drive them even further apart. My non-Jewish husband is the definition of an upstander and the ally every Jew needs. My heart almost left my chest when I heard him say in our meeting: 'I believe that right now, antisemitism is the number one race discrimination issue globally, and we need more Holocaust education in our schools.'

In response, the school said they were looking to invite a Jewish speaker to address the students. Knowing that Ittay would be coming to Perth for his book launch, I suggested they invite him to address the students and the wider school community. Both the school and Ittay agreed. My son's face lit up when I told him that the unacceptable hatred he has faced since October 7 would not be in vain, and that we would soon meet Ittay in person.

My friendship circle has expanded in yet other ways. For most of my adulthood, I've felt isolated as a Jew in Perth – until this year, I only knew one other Jewish person in my postcode. Most of my friends are part of the silent majority of Australians who abhor antisemitism. Some have reached out to express their dismay at what has happened to my son and the brazen displays of Jew-hatred in Australia. But as kind and empathetic as they are, I realise it's impossible for them to understand the visceral fear their Jewish friends have been feeling since October 7, and how the Israel-Hamas war is impacting our daily lives.

That's also why the message from my friend in Los Angeles, where he called on me to 'feed the joy and the love and the companionship that come from being part of the Jewish community' struck such a chord.

I knew it would soothe me to be around people who implicitly understood the heaviness I felt. Through social media, I've connected with other Jewish writers, and I'm also now part of a self-described 'Chutzpah Club' of Jewish mothers, which I formed with the only Jewish mother I know from my son's school, one of her school friends, and the Jewish neighbour I recently discovered on my street. We've gone out for drinks and dinner, and every few weeks we take turns driving to the northern suburbs for our kosher bagel and challah fix. Our Jewish neighbours recently joined my family for Shabbat dinner – a lowkey and cheerful affair where our children lit the Shabbat candles and recited blessings for the wine and challah in broken Hebrew.

While there are miles separating Perth and Los Angeles, my friend's voice message will stay with me: *Step out of the negativity and show people you are about love. And if they still hate you, it's a reflection of them, not you.*

I am taking his wise advice and choosing to focus on the meaningful connections I've made since October 7 that have kept me afloat during the darkest hours, when I can't stop thinking about all the victims of this war, the hostages and the future my sons will face as Jews in Australia. These connections remind me that despite the odds stacked against those of us who believe that peace is still possible, we are strong and vital links in a growing chain of hope. And they emerged at a time when I needed them most.

As for my dear friend across the oceans, the answer is yes, our friendship can take it.

I'M NOT ANTISEMITIC, BUT...

RACHELLE UNREICH

I am pleased when I receive the invitation to a writers festival held in a little regional town. I have been asked to interview one of my favourite authors about her new book. I am also glad to be returning to this particular town in Victoria, since it is a place I holidayed at with my parents when I was little. My recollections of it are soaked in retro 1970s nostalgia: we would drive there in my father's aqua blue Holden station wagon, a mattress squeezed into the boot so I could read over the long drive. Once, we stayed in a local pub and a drunken guy started yelling outside our door. My father – broad and strong, an ex-wrestler – told him to pipe down, not the least bit intimidated. This should be a bad memory but it's not. It reminds me how safe I felt under my parents' protection, no matter the threat.

The festival organisers tell me that they will also be promoting my memoir, *A Brilliant Life*, which is about my late mother Mira, a Holocaust survivor. She had died by the time I started writing it, but she must have suspected it would come to fruition one day; I had been a working journalist since my late teens, and sometimes

I would tell her of my plans to put her story to paper. 'That's okay, I'll be dead!' she'd say with a laugh – a line which was so typical of both her laissez-faire attitude and her humour. She was seventeen when she entered the first of four concentration camps she'd endure, including Auschwitz which she exited on a death march. Yet after the war she lived her life joyfully. When she died at the age of 89, I started penning her story as a way to unfurl the curled fingers of loss that dug into my sides. In writing, I transformed my grief into something else: connection.

That connection has helped me through the devastating post-October 7 days. *A Brilliant Life* came out in Australia just three weeks after the massacre, and hit bookstores around the world not long after that. Since then, my native city of Melbourne has seen the rising tide of antisemitism take hold; there have been protests, university encampments, ugly graffiti on residential homes. But even though security is heightened at my book events, what I mainly feel is support from strangers. They arrive at my talks and present me with offerings: home-made jams and treats, and, more often than not, replicas of food items mentioned in my book. At a country women's luncheon, a woman had baked a sweet challah loaf, having watched how to do so on YouTube, painting the crust with egg so that the top glistened. On several occasions, readers have presented me with the almond horseshoe biscuits that Mira made, sourcing the recipe from Eastern European cookbooks. A woman in America sent me a soft bookmark she made from suede; on it, she embroidered a blue bird, referring to the fact that whenever I see a blue-coloured bird now, I am convinced it is my mother Mira sending me a sign. None of the people who have brought these gifts have been Jewish, but they share something else in common with my mother: empathy, generosity, kindness.

However, my mother's story doesn't always move people for the better. At the aforementioned Victorian festival, I am prepared for the interview; I have gone over my questions and read the author's book three times. The author is somewhat nervous – in the green room she confides that she doesn't like doing publicity. But I am not. I have become accustomed to crowds, to audiences, to bright lights shining on me, keeping the rest of the room shrouded in darkness. We begin, and she soon relaxes; my work has paid off. I check my watch at the thirty-five minute mark, knowing that soon I will open up the floor to questions. We are in the home stretch.

And then: a man jumps onto the stage. I cannot see his face; he is directing his monologue to the audience, and all I see is his back, the light bouncing off his long, blonde hair. 'Let me tell you a story about Gaza,' he tells the audience. My brain is still processing what has summoned him here, trying to calculate the level of threat. Is he armed? I think I hear a few groans in the audience, but nobody makes a move, and the man continues his speech.

Holding my microphone, I try to speak over him as it dawns on me – slowly – what is happening. 'Oh. Sorry,' I tell the crowd. 'He's here because of me. *Because I am Jewish*. And even though I have not written a book about Israel or the Middle East, he thinks it's okay to disrupt a stage I'm on. Because I'm Jewish.' I don't know if I really say all of this in this way, but some of it certainly comes tumbling out. Nevertheless, it is impossible to drown him out: he is determined and loud, even without sound equipment.

I wait for security to haul him offstage, but it is only after many minutes that someone gently commandeers him to the side and escorts him out. The author asks me if I am okay, and I tell her I am. 'My people have had to deal with worse than this guy,' I say, and it is true. But my bluster soon fades; I am already going through the 'what if' scenarios. What if he had a knife? What if he had attacked me? The scenes that would have seemed paranoid and hysterical a year ago are no longer that, in this surreal present day.

I finish the session, and stumble off the stage to sign books. People nod and smile at me as they file past. 'You handled that so well!' they say cheerily. The organisers feel bad for me and want to be reassured that I am all right, but I'm not sure they each felt the threat of the moment, or the way it felt like an assault. Some are already tempering the moment with words.

'He's a real firebrand, that kid,' one says. It turns out the protestor is a school student; from the back, I had pegged him as being in his twenties.

'Everyone has a side, don't they,' another adds.

But is it really so? I have not taken any sides in any war. Until now, I have taken pains to avoid political talk. I am not an expert on the Middle East. All I want to do is tell my mother's story. Ironically, her message is one that suits this turn of events, and in my concluding address to the audience, I offered some of it. That lumping people into a category allows no room for nuance or understanding, but instead paves the way for hate, division and violence. If she were alive, my mother might have spoken about the need for critical thinking and compassion. One must never forget one's humanity. Mira's parents, her only sister and her youngest brother were murdered in the Holocaust, and still she said, 'In the Holocaust, I learned about the goodness of people.' She did not focus on the cruelty she had seen; she chose to remember, instead, those who had helped her, risked their lives for her, saved her.

***

It's not long before I receive my first piece of hate mail. It snakes into my inbox two hours after an essay I've written appears online – a piece about being Jewish and trying to combat antisemitism. The sender tells me I am participating in a genocide. She ends her letter with three exclamation marks as if to underscore the veracity of her message. It is not anonymous; she has included her name, and when I look her up, I see the photo of a woman who is grey-haired, teetering towards old age. It is hard to believe this stranger holds so much hatred towards me. 'I am not antisemitic…' is the opening line of her letter, and this little phrase is followed immediately by the word 'but'. A psychologist once told me that it's a word that often negates everything that comes before it. 'I love you, but…' 'I'm sorry, but…'

My heart beats fast when I read this missive; I can't be indifferent to it. For days, I toy with a possible response. Do I call her, to see what she says when confronted with me, an actual person? My friends tell me I shouldn't bother, for what will it achieve?

Perhaps they are right. I am accustomed to words being my tool – to alleviate trouble, to express love and sympathy. But now, all around me, words I am familiar with have taken on distorted meanings and it's as if I need a new dictionary that redefines their regular meanings. Genocide. Zionist. I'm Not Antisemitic But. These words are spat out – another weapon in war.

As a writer, I cannot stop believing in the power of language. But now I understand the importance of action too. How different it might have been if, at that festival, the audience members had risen to their feet to help me.

Still, words also helped. After the event, one of the organisers invited me to tell the festival team how I felt. They all listened attentively as I spoke to that, including how I'd been feeling for months. How this persistent antisemitism had covered so much of my world with its ugliness. How it had made me scared, yes, but also how it had made me feel more connected to my community, my history, my ancestors. To the readers around me who, upon finishing my mother's story, reach out and send me messages of solidarity. 'I now have a new and profound interest in Judaism,' writes Savannah from the US. 'Sending you love and support in this terrible time,' says Rae in Canberra. I hear from people in far-flung countries: Switzerland, Germany, Israel. From all over the world, they find their way to my inbox to say the same thing: you are not alone. I try to believe this for, like Mira, I know that human goodness is more powerful than hate. And that what makes a difference to us, Jews, are those who speak up in solidarity. Those who take on 'Never Again' as their motto too.

CONTRIBUTORS

Dani Valent is a writer based in Melbourne. Known mostly for her food writing and restaurant reviews for *The Age*, she is also a longtime feature and travel writer, and speaker and host of the *Dirty Linen* podcast.

Deborah Conway AM has been a recording and performing musician for over 40 years; a producer, festival director, actor and author of the memoir *Book of Life*. She is a recipient of the Don Banks Award given for outstanding contribution to music and has been inducted into Music Victoria's Hall of Fame.

Dena Amy Kaplan, known as **Dena Amy**, is an actress, dancer, artist and international touring DJ. Recognised for her roles in *Dance Academy*, *Long Story Short* and *Occupation Rainfall*, she blends performance with music, captivating audiences worldwide. A passionate advocate for mental health and the arts, she champions creativity as a force for empowerment and connection.

CONTRIBUTORS

Elana Benjamin is a Jewish-Australian writer of Indian-Iraqi heritage. Her work has been published widely, including in *Good Weekend, Sunday Life*, the *Sydney Morning Herald, SBS Voices* and *The Jewish Independent*. Elana's most recent book is *Indian-Jewish Food: Recipes and stories from the backstreets of Bondi* (2024, Sydney Jewish Museum).

Elise Esther Hearst is an award-winning writer and performer living on Boonwurrung country. Her novel, *One Day We're All Going to Die*, was shortlisted for The Age Book of the Year Award 2024. Her theatre work has been performed across Australia, including at the Sydney Opera House and with the Melbourne Theatre Company. Find her on Instagram @eliseestherhearst

Galit Klas is a playwright and performer based in Melbourne. She has combined her passion for Yiddish language and theatre in works such as *Yentl, The Ghetto Cabaret,* and *Durkh a Modne Gloz*. Galit is also the founding artistic director of the Kadimah Yiddish Theatre.

Irena Zilberman was born in Ukraine and emigrated to Australia with her family in 1992. She has a Bachelor of Creative Arts and a Master of Counselling. Irena works as a grief and trauma counsellor, and lives with her two adorable cats Maple and Butterscotch.

Rabbi Jacqueline Ninio OAM was ordained as a rabbi in 1998. She was the third Australian woman to be ordained as a rabbi and the first at Emanuel Synagogue in Sydney. Rabbi Ninio has an Honorary Doctorate of Divinity and an OAM for her services to the Jewish community and interfaith dialogue.

Jemima Montag is an Olympic medallist, medical student and keynote speaker. She attributes her strength and determination to her two late grandparents who were Holocaust survivors.

Jessica Bowker is a writer and corporate communications consultant in Perth, Western Australia. A member of the Fellowship of Australian Writers WA, she writes with the Indian Ocean Writers' Group. Her creative non-fiction works are published in *The Jewish Independent* and in the *Ourselves:100 Micro Memoirs* anthology.

Joanne Fedler is the internationally bestselling author of fifteen books, a writing mentor, publisher and open water swimmer. She is a Fulbright scholar, has a master's degree in law from Yale, and was a women's rights advocate before she became a full-time author.

Julia Meyerowitz-Katz is a Sydney-based Jungian psychoanalyst, art psychotherapist and artist. Published in books and journals, Julia specialises in working with adults and couples who present with complex trauma. Art-making has been a life-long preoccupation for Julia; she has exhibited her artwork in Australia and internationally.

Julie Szego is an author and freelance writer. A former journalist at *The Age*, her work has been widely published in Australian and overseas media. She writes a Substack newsletter, *SzegoUnplugged*.

Kate Lewis is mother, interior architect and occasional writer. Creative, connected and, when necessary, confrontational.

Kerri Sackville is a Sydney-based author, columnist and social commentator. She has written five works of non-fiction and contributed to three anthologies. Her latest book is *The Secret Life of You: How a bit of alone time can change your life, relationships, and maybe the world* (Pantera Press). Website: kerrisackville.com.au

CONTRIBUTORS

Professor Kim Rubenstein is a Fellow of the Australian Academy of Law and the Australian Academy of Social Sciences. An expert in all things citizenship, she was awarded the 2024 Council of Australian Law Dean's Lifetime Achievement Medal for her significant and impactful contributions to legal research in Australia.

Kylie Moore-Gilbert is an academic, writer and human rights advocate based in Melbourne. She is the author of the bestselling 2022 memoir *The Uncaged Sky: My 804 days in an Iranian prison* and is the founding director of the Australian Wrongful and Arbitrary Detention Alliance.

Lana Schwarcz has been a comic performer, puppeteer and 'theatre-maker' for 30-something years. After October 7, she left the creative sector for a new career in emergency management but, ironically, has just been nominated for a Green Room Award for her last theatre show about abortion, *The Term-inator*.

Dr Lee Kofman is the Israeli-Australian author of eight books in English and Hebrew, including *Imperfect* (Affirm Press), which was shortlisted for a Nib Literary Award, *Split* (Ventura Press), which was longlisted for ABIA and the writing book, *The Writer Laid Bare* (Ventura Press). She has been teaching and mentoring writers for over twenty years.

Lisa Goldberg co-founded the Monday Morning Cooking Club project to document and preserve recipes and stories from Jewish kitchens, publishing four cookbooks. A fifth book, for the next generation, will be released in 2026. Lisa has a YouTube food show, *Walking up an Appetite*, and has become a social media advocate for the Jewish community.

Lynette Chazan is a psychiatrist and psychoanalytic psychotherapist in private practice. She teaches, supervises, and has published on psychotherapy training, developmental trauma, doctors' wellbeing and Palestinian/Israeli dialogue. She would have liked to write more, but finds it too difficult.

Melinda Jones is a pioneering legal scholar who has shaped human rights, administrative law and disability inclusion. A thought leader, she has worked to advance women's roles in Modern Orthodox Judaism and the inclusion of Jews with disabilities in the community. She has authored eleven books and more than 50 articles influencing law, policy and social justice.

Dr Mindy Sotiri has worked in criminal justice system settings as an advocate, community sector practitioner, activist, academic and researcher for more than twenty-five years. She is also a musician and songwriter and has released five albums over the last twenty years.

Nicky Stein is a lawyer, wife, mother and accidental advocate. As a child, she aspired to write but never expected her first publication would be in response to antisemitism. She is honoured to appear in this book with incredible Jewish women's voices.

Nina Sanadze, a Soviet-born, Melbourne-based visual artist and sculptor, explores monuments, archives and political action. Her work constructs a wall of remembrance to resist repeating histories or war. She recently opened Goldstone Gallery, providing a platform for silenced voices, including cancelled Jewish and Israeli artists, and those facing censorship.

Noa Gomberg is a high school student who loves making readers feel the impact of her words. She also may or may not have ignored the rule that only adult women could submit to this anthology.

Noè Harsel is a writer, podcaster and arts leader. She hosts the podcasts *Why Write* and *Like Us* (SBS), was chair of Writers Victoria and is the former director and CEO of the Jewish Museum of Australia. Noè is committed to fostering inclusive creative spaces through writing, public speaking and cultural advocacy.

Rachelle Unreich has worked as a journalist for 40 years. Her first book, *A Brilliant Life: My mother's inspiring story of surviving the Holocaust*, was shortlisted for four literary awards and has been published in Australia/NZ, USA/Canada, UK, South Africa and The Netherlands.

Ramona Koval is a writer and journalist, author of *A Letter to Layla: Travels to our deep past and near future* (Text, 2020), *Bloodhound* (Text, 2015), *By the Book* (Text, 2012) and *Speaking Volumes: Interviews with remarkable writers* (Scribe, 2010). She is an honorary fellow in the Department of Communication and Creative Arts, Deakin University.

Ruby Kraner-Tucci is a journalist and assistant editor at *The Jewish Independent*. Her writing has appeared in *The Age*, *Australian Jewish News* and *Broadsheet*, among others. Ruby's column won Multicultural NSW's Best Report in Multicultural Media (2025) and she was named a B'nai Brith-JNF Top 36 Under 36 Jewish Changemaker.

Sharon Sztar is an ex-corporate communications executive turned writer and women's wellbeing advocate. Melbourne-born and bred, Sharon is now based in the NSW Northern Rivers region. Her work and writing explore and challenge the narratives of what it means to be a well woman across all seasons of life.

Sharonne Blum has been a Jewish studies educator for over twenty years. She is a proud Jew, Zionist and dual Australian-Israeli citizen. After October 7, she embraced a new role as an advocate and activist for her people and culture.

Siana Einfeld is a teacher librarian and storyteller living in Melbourne. She is currently writing a young adult novel set in her ideal habitat: between the forest and the sea.

Sidra Kranz Moshinsky is a writer, researcher and educational leader. Having taught and led in Jewish education for over fifteen years, she is now engaged in projects at the Jewish Museum of Australia, JCCV and the Jewish Educators Network of Australia. She is a contributor to *The Jewish Independent* and a board member of Kolenu.

Simonne Whine is a project manager turned accidental activist. In the wake of October 7, she founded J-United, a grassroots activist movement mobilising thousands to combat antisemitism and strengthen Jewish identity. Through strategic action she has created platforms for unity, advocacy and empowerment, inspiring others to stand up and take action.

Tamar Paluch trained as an occupational therapist, with a focus on disability rights and community development. October 7 drew her into women-led activism and rekindled her writing practice. Together with her husband and two daughters, she has lived in Tel Aviv, New York City, Melbourne and now Los Angeles.

ACKNOWLEDGEMENTS

This book represents one small attempt to mend the rupture of these times, and it has been a great honour to work on it together and with the support of many others.

First of all, our deepest gratitude goes to Romy Moshinsky, whose editorial input and publishing nous were invaluable; and to Simonne Whine, who has overseen the project management with vision and finesse. Without the two of you, this book would have never happened.

To our contributors – it has been a privilege to work with you, particularly considering the high stakes for all involved and the inhospitable cultural and social landscape we find ourselves in. We are so grateful for your tenacity and willingness to share your stories to illuminate the Jewish experience as we live it.

We would like to thank Dr Rolene Lamm, chair of the Lamm Jewish Library of Australia, for giving this project a home and publishing these stories as part of their commitment to storytelling and community, and to Dr Merav Carmeli for her constant support and dedication to the project. We are also deeply grateful to Richard Leder OAM of Wotton Kearney for his ongoing commitment to this book. Thank you for understanding and acting on the urgency of writing this chapter in Jewish history.

To those who gave their expertise and time in support of the anthology project, warmest thanks to: Trudi Arnold, Roz Bellamy, Marianna Berek-Lewis, Annette Cohen, Deborah Conway AM, Jane Curry, Paula Darvas, Nadine Davidoff, Karen Diamond, Sheila Esterman, Michael Gawenda, Dmetri Kakmi, Leah Kaminsky, Kathy Kaplan, Ramona Koval, Jeremy Leibler and ABL, Laini Liberman, Georgie Raik-Allen, Rina Retman, Danielle Reznick Jones, Professor Kim Rubenstein, Melinda Tassone, Simon Tedeschi, Maggie Walters, Suzy Zail and Elahn Zetlin.

A big thank you to Van Badham, Nina Bassat AM, Robyn Cadwallader, Yvette Henry Holt, Meg Kenneally, Professor Catharine Lumby, Julie McCrossin AM, Nova Peris OAM OLY and Alice Zaslavsky who generously took the time to read and provide thoughtful endorsements. We thank Morry Schwartz for his encouragement and for supporting Jewish writers in these challenging times. And thank you to our wonderful PR powerhouse Deb McInnes and her expert team for all their hard work promoting *Ruptured*.

This anthology has its roots in the InternationALL Women's Day Platform, co-founded in March 2024 by Susie Ivany OAM, Kylie Appel and Tamar Paluch to help Jewish women reclaim their narratives and document history in the aftermath of October 7. Together with Simonne Whine and Romy Moshinsky, and in partnership with Dr Rolene Lamm and Dr Merav Carmeli at LJLA, we invited Jewish women to reflect on 'A Year Like No Other', and how this seminal event impacted on life in Australia. We received close to 150 essays and the full collection will be preserved for the

ACKNOWLEDGEMENTS

historical record in the National Library of Israel October 7 Archive and in the archive of Lamm Jewish Library of Australia. Most of the essays featured in Ruptured were selected from those submissions.

We would like to extend our deep gratitude to all the women who contributed their stories to this platform. To the women who believed in and funded our initiative and the publication of this book, we are immensely grateful for your generosity – in particular: the 6A Foundation, Ben Zeev family, Brass Family Trust, Caulfield Park Community Financial Services Limited, Debbie Dadon AM, Janet Hiller, Susie Ivany OAM and Paul Ivany, Romy Moshinsky, Pauline Rockman OAM and Avi Paluch, Ricci Swart, and Simonne Whine.

Thank you to all the professionals, creatives, mums and grandmas-turned-activists who seeded the InternationALL Women's Day platform and so many other invaluable grassroots efforts that have strengthened our community during these difficult times. We have seen you doing the hard work of preserving our past and securing our future, and we hope you feel represented in these pages.

Finally, on a personal note, all our gratitude and love to our patient husbands, Daryl Efron and Shilo Ben Zeev, and our (less patient) children Luca, Ollie, Amalia and Rahni, who put up with their preoccupied wives and mothers for the many months and hours that it took us to compile this book.

Photo credit: Markus Stone

Dr Lee Kofman is the author of six books, including a book on writing, *The Writer Laid Bare* (Ventura Press, 2022), memoirs *Imperfect* (Affirm Press, 2019), which was shortlisted for Nib Literary Award, and *The Dangerous Bride* (Melbourne University Press, 2014). She is the co-editor of *Rebellious Daughters* (Ventura Press, 2016) and editor of *Split* (Ventura Press, 2019), which was longlisted for ABIA Awards – anthologies of memoir by prominent Australian authors. Her short works have been widely published in Australia and overseas. Lee regularly speaks at literary events, judges literary awards, and is an experienced writing mentor and teacher.

Tamar Paluch trained as an occupational therapist, with a focus on disability rights and community development. October 7 drew her into women-led activism, and she co-founded the InternationALL Women's Day platform and the community writing initiative 'A Year Like No Other' as a way to document history and help women reclaim their voice in these complex times. *Ruptured* is a culmination of these initiatives and her long-held passion for writing and editing, especially on matters of grief, identity and memory. Together with her husband and two daughters, she has lived in Tel Aviv, New York City, Melbourne and Los Angeles.